MANDARIN
*go*Chinese

· ·

Speak & Learn the Pimsleur® Way

Culture Notes

SIMON & SCHUSTER'S
PIMSLEUR

Hear it, Learn it, Speak it

03744816

For more information, call
1-800-831-5497 or visit us
at www.Pimsleur.com

Graphic Design: Maia Kennedy

goChinese · Mandarin

ACKNOWLEDGMENTS

VOICES

English-Speaking Instructor . . . . *Ray Brown*
Female Mandarin Speaker. . . . . *Mei Ling Diep*
Male Mandarin Speaker . . . . *Yaohua Shi*

COURSE WRITERS
Mei Ling Diep (I)   ♦   Yaohua Shi (II & III)
Christopher J. Gainty

EDITORS
Kimiko Ise Abramoff (I)   ♦   Joan Schoellner (II & III)

EDITOR & EXECUTIVE PRODUCER
Beverly D. Heinle

PRODUCER & DIRECTOR
Sarah H. McInnis

RECORDING ENGINEERS
Peter S. Turpin   •   Kelly Saux

Simon & Schuster Studios, Concord, MA

iii

goChinese · Mandarin

TABLE OF CONTENTS

Travelers should always check with their nation's State Department for current advisories on local conditions before traveling abroad.

Introduction

• •

You have just purchased the most effective language program ever developed. As you probably know, learning a new language can be frustrating. Your first experience with a foreign language may have been in school. If the classes seemed difficult, or if your grades were poor, you probably believed you had no aptitude for languages. Even if you did well, you may have been surprised later to discover that what you learned was of little or no use when you tried to converse with native speakers.

Perhaps you waited until later in life and tried adult education classes, language schools, or home training programs. There too you may have found the information hard to retain, the lessons tedious, and your progress slow. Many language students give up early in these programs, convinced they lack the natural ability to understand and use what they read and hear.

The truth is that anyone can acquire a foreign language — with the right teaching system. With the Pimsleur® Method, you will benefit from the years of research and development that have helped create the world's most effective method for teaching foreign languages. The Pimsleur® Language Programs, developed by Dr. Paul Pimsleur, fill an urgent need for self-instructional materials in many languages.

How to Use the Program
• •

To get the full benefit of each lesson, choose a quiet place where you can practice without interruption and a time of day when your mind is most alert and your body least fatigued.

The length of each lesson, just under 30 minutes, is that recommended by teaching specialists for a concentrated learning task. Once you've started the program, simply follow the tutor's instructions. The most important instruction is to respond aloud when the tutor tells you to do so. There will be a pause after this instruction, giving you time to reply. It is essential to your progress that you speak out in a normal conversational voice when asked to respond. Your active participation in thinking and speaking is required for your success in mastering this course.

The simple test for mastery is whether you are able to respond quickly and accurately when your tutor asks a question. If you are responding correctly about eighty percent of the time, then you're ready to proceed to the next lesson. It is important to keep moving forward, and also not to set unreasonable standards of perfection that will keep you from progressing, which is why we recommend using the eighty percent figure as a guide.

• •

You will notice that each lesson contains both new and familiar material, and just when you may be worrying about forgetting something, you will conveniently be reminded of it. Another helpful feature of the Pimsleur® Language Program is its rate of "saturation." You will be responding many times in the half-hour. This saturation enables you to make substantial progress within a short period of time.

Guidelines for Success

Complete the lesson units in strict consecutive order (don't skip around), doing no more than one lesson per day, although the lesson unit for the day may be repeated more than once. Daily contact with the language is critical to successful learning.

Listen carefully to each lesson unit. Always follow the directions of the tutor.

Speak out loud when directed by the tutor and answer questions within the pauses provided. It is not enough to just silently "think" of the answer to the question asked. You need to speak the answer out loud to set up a "circuit" of the language you are learning to speak so that it is heard and identified through your ears, to help to establish the "sounds"

• •

of the target language. Do this prior to hearing the confirmation, which is provided as reinforcement, as well as additional speech training.

Do all required activities according to the instructions, without reference to any outside persons, text-books, or courses.

Do not have a paper and pen nearby during the lessons, and do not refer to dictionaries or other text-books while doing the spoken lessons. The Pimsleur® Method works with the language-learning portion of your brain, requiring language to be processed in its spoken form. Not only will you interrupt the learning process if you attempt to write the words that you hear before learning to read in the new language, but you will also begin to speak the target language with an American accent. This is because the sounds represented by the American letters are frequently different from the sounds of the same-looking letters in the foreign language.

Dr. Paul Pimsleur

Dr. Paul Pimsleur devoted his life to language teaching and testing and was one of the world's leading experts in applied linguistics. He was fluent

• •

in French, good in German, and had a working knowledge of Italian, Russian, Modern Greek, and Mandarin Chinese. After obtaining his Ph.D. in French and a Masters in Psychology from Columbia University, he taught French Phonetics and Linguistics at UCLA. He later became Professor of Romance Languages and Language Education, and Director of The Listening Center (a state-wide language lab) at Ohio State University; Professor of Education and Romance Languages at the State University of New York at Albany; and a Fulbright lecturer at the University of Heidelberg.

Dr. Pimsleur was a founding member of the American Council on the Teaching of Foreign Languages (ACTFL). His many books and articles revolutionized theories of language learning and teaching. After years of experience and research, Dr. Pimsleur developed a new method (The Pimsleur® Method) that is based on two key principles: the *Principle of Anticipation*™ and a scientific principle of memory training that he called *Graduated Interval Recall*™. This Method has been applied to the many levels and languages of the Pimsleur® Programs.

Graduated Interval Recall™

• •

Graduated Interval Recall™ is a complex name for a very simple theory about memory. No aspect of learning a foreign language is more important than memory, yet before Dr. Pimsleur, no one had explored more effective ways for building language memory.

In his research, Dr. Pimsleur discovered how long students remembered new information and at what intervals they needed to be reminded of it. If reminded too soon or too late, they failed to retain the information. This discovery enabled him to create a schedule of exactly when and how the information should be reintroduced.

Suppose you have learned a new word. You tell yourself to remember it. However, after five minutes you're unable to recall it. If you'd been reminded of it after five seconds, you probably would have remembered it for maybe a minute, at which time you would have needed another reminder. Each time you are reminded, you remember the word longer than you did the time before. The intervals between reminders become longer and longer, until you eventually remember the word without being reminded at all.

Graduated Interval Recall™ (continued)
• •

This program is carefully designed to remind you of new information at the exact intervals where maximum retention takes place. Each time your memory begins to fade, you will be asked to recall the word.

Principle of Anticipation™

The *Principle of Anticipation*™ requires you to anticipate a correct answer. Practically, what this means is that you must retrieve the answer from what you have learned earlier in the course. It works by posing a question, asking you to provide a new sentence, using information you've learned previously and putting it into a new combination. This provides novelty and excitement which accelerates learning.

A possible scenario:

Speaker's cue: "Are you going to the movies today?"
--- PAUSE ---
Drawing on information given previously, you respond *(in the target language)*: "No, I'm going tomorrow."
The instructor will then confirm your answer:
"No, I'm going tomorrow."

• •

The Narrator then may cue:
"Is your sister going to Europe this year?"
--- PAUSE ---
Response: "No, she went last year."

Before Dr. Pimsleur created his teaching meth-od, language courses were based on the principle of "mindless-repetition." Teachers monotonously drummed words into the students' minds, as if there were grooves in the mind that could be worn deeper with repetition.

Neurophysiologists tell us however, that on the contrary, simple and unchallenging repetition has a hypnotic, even dulling effect on the learning process. Eventually, the words being repeated will lose their meaning. Dr. Pimsleur discovered that learning ac-celerates when there is an "input/output" system of interaction, in which students receive information and then are asked to retrieve and use it.

Core Vocabulary

While *Graduated Interval Recall*™ and the *Prin-ciple of Anticipation*™ are the foundation of the Pimsleur® Method, there are other aspects that con-tribute to its uniqueness and effectiveness. One involves vocabulary. We have all been intimidated,

Core Vocabulary (continued)

• •

when approaching a new language, by the sheer immensity of the number of new words we must learn. But extensive research has shown that we actually need a comparatively limited number of words to be able to communicate effectively in any language.

Language can be divided into two distinct categories: grammatical structures (function words) and concrete vocabulary (content words). By focusing on the former category and enabling the student to comprehend and employ the structure of the new language, Dr. Pimsleur found that language learners were able to more readily put new knowledge to use. There are few content words that must be known and used every day. The essential "core" of a language involves function words, which tend to relate to human activities.

This course is designed to teach you to understand and to speak the essential elements of your new language in a relatively short time. During each half-hour lesson, you will actually converse with two native speakers, using the level of language spoken by educated citizens in their everyday business and social life. The program's unique method of presenting dialogue in-situation relieves you of the most common learning problem, the problem of meaning.

Organic Learning
• •

The Pimsleur® Method centers on teaching functional mastery in understanding and speaking a language, in the most effective and efficient way possible. You will be working on your vocabulary, grammar, and pronunciation in an integrated manner, as you are learning specific phrases that have practical use in everyday activities.

There are several thousand languages in the world. Because fewer than five hundred of these languages have developed formal systems of writing, linguistic specialists accept that language is primarily speech. For this reason, it is also accepted that the human brain acquires language as speech. Therefore, when Dr. Pimsleur created his language programs, he began teaching with recorded materials, which enabled the learners to acquire the sounds, the rhythm, and the intonation of the target language. The learners did this more rapidly, more accurately, and with great enthusiasm because they found themselves capable of almost instant beginning communication skills.

Dr. Pimsleur called this "organic learning" because it involves learning on several fronts at the same time. His system enables the learner to acquire grammatical usage, vocabulary, and the sounds of the language in an integrated, exciting

• •

way. In short, the learner gains the language as a living, expressive form of human culture.

Course Content

When you have mastered a Pimsleur® Language Program, you will have a highly practical, everyday vocabulary at your command. These basic words, phrases, and sentences have been carefully selected to be the most useful in everyday situations when you visit a foreign country. You will be able to handle social encounters graciously, converse with native speakers intravel situations, and use transportation systems with confidence. You'll be able to ask directions and to navigate your own way around the cities and countryside.

The language skills you learn will enable you to participate in casual conversations, express facts, give instructions, and describe current, past, and future activities. You will be able to deal with everyday survival topics and courtesy requirements. You will be intelligible to native speakers of the language — even to those who are not used to dealing with foreigners. What is equally important, you will know how to ask the kinds of questions that will further expand your knowledge of and facility with the

• •

language, because you will have been trained by the Pimsleur® open-ended questioning technique.

The Pimsleur® Method becomes a springboard for further learning and growth to take place — the ultimate purpose of any real educational system. This desire to learn will be apparent to the people with whom you speak. It will indicate sincere interest in and respect for their culture.

In any large country, and even in many smaller countries, regional differences in language are common. In the United States, for example, a person from Maine can sound very different than someone from Texas. Pronunciations ("accents") vary, and there are also minor differences in vocabulary. For example, what is called a "drinking fountain" in New York or Arizona is known as a "bubbler" in Wisconsin, and a "soft drink" in one part of America will be called a "soda" elsewhere. The differences in English are even more distinct between North Americans and Britons, or between Britons and Australians. But all are native speakers of English; all can communicate with spoken English, read the same newspapers, and watch the same television programs, essentially without difficulty.

Native speakers of a language can often tell where someone is from by listening to him or her speak. In addition to regional differences, there are social differences. Pimsleur® Language Programs use a standard "educated" speech, which will generally carry you throughout the country without difficulty.

MANDARIN

goChinese

· ·

Speak & Learn the Pimsleur® Way

Culture Notes

PART ONE

Part One *go*Chinese · Mandarin

TABLE OF CONTENTS
• •

Introduction
● ●

Learning any language is enhanced by some knowledge of the cultural customs and beliefs of its native speakers. Developing an awareness of and a sensitivity to a language's subtleties are inherent to acquiring true fluency. The following "Notes" for Pimsleur's *Mandarin I* are meant to provide you with an introduction as to how the language and the culture are intertwined.

The Mandarin Language

Mandarin is standard spoken Chinese, used by the government, in the schools, and on radio and TV broadcasts. Although there are eight major Chinese dialects, Mandarin is native to approximately seventy percent of the population and is the only dialect that has a corresponding written form of the language. Chinese who are educated through at least the primary grades speak Mandarin as well as local dialects. However, due to the size of China and the ethnic diversity of its inhabitants, hundreds of other dialects are spoken in different areas. The dialects spoken today are based more on geography than on ethnicity. For instance, residents of Shanghai will speak *wu*. In some parts of China, particularly the central and southern areas, education and official business are transacted in the locally dominant language. Although people from different parts of China may not understand one another's spoken language, they use the same basic set of characters for writing.

Today's Mandarin is closely based on "northern speech" which was the lingua franca of the ruling class, spoken in Beijing, the capital during the Yuan, Ming and Qing Dynasties. After the Qing Dynasty collapsed in 1912, the new Republic government decided to retain Mandarin as the "National Language," *guo yu* in Chinese. The Communists, who defeated the Nationalists in 1949, continued this policy, but they changed the name and coined the term *pu tong hua* or "common speech" for "Mandarin." This is the word for Mandarin used throughout mainland China. In Hong Kong, however, as in Taiwan and most overseas communities, *guo yu*, the older term, continues to be used.

Chinese Characters
• •

Traditionally, Chinese characters are divided into six different categories. It is commonly thought that every Chinese character is a picture, or "pictograph," but only a few hundred of the several thousand characters are true pictographs. However, most of these are now written in such a way that it is difficult to immediately guess their meaning. There is also a very small group of characters called "ideographs" or "ideograms," which represent ideas or objects directly. An example would be the character for blade. It is based on the pictograph for knife with the addition of an extra stroke marking the blade.

Ideograms and pictographs can be combined to form associative compounds, for instance, doubling the pictograph for tree to mean woods. A fourth category is comprised of phonetic loan characters. There is also a fifth category with a very small number of modified cognates, characters that have taken on different forms through orthographic and semantic changes. However, by far the most significant category is the so-called phono-semantic compounds, meaning the characters combine phonetic as well as semantic clues. These represent about 90% of the characters in use today.

Traditional and Simplified Script

• •

In the 1950s, in order to promote literacy, the Chinese government decided to "simplify" the existing characters by reducing the number of strokes necessary to create them. By 1964, a list of 2,238 simplified characters was created. Further simplification was briefly adopted, then quickly abandoned in the 1970s.

Presently, simplified characters are used in mainland China and Singapore. Hong Kong, Taiwan, and most overseas Chinese communities continue to use the traditional characters.

Tonality

Chinese is a monosyllabic language with an abundance of homonyms. The tone with which a syllable is pronounced helps to determine its meaning. Each tone has a name which describes the relative pitch of the main vowel. In this way, several meanings can be assigned to any one syllable, depending on the tone with which it is pronounced. For example, when pronounced using a falling-rising tone, the word *nar* means "where." However, when this word is pronounced with just a falling tone, *nar,* it means "there."

Tonality (continued)

• •

There are four basic tones in Mandarin: high level, rising, falling-rising, and falling. In addition, there is a "soft" sound which is used for the second syllable of certain compound words, as well as particles, words that convey grammatical and other meanings. The soft tone is also known as the neutral tone since its pitch contour is determined by the preceding tone.

Here is an example of one sound with several possible meanings, depending on the tone with which it is pronounced:

1st tone	2nd tone
High	**Rising**
shi ("poem")	*shi* ("ten")

3rd tone	4th tone
Falling-rising	**Falling**
shi ("history")	*shi* (all the forms of "to be")

Remember that Chinese is rich in homonyms, which means a single syllable can take many different written forms and convey different meanings.

Tone Change

• •

Although each Chinese syllable standing alone has a specific tone, in the flow of speech the tone of a syllable can change depending on the tone of the following syllable. In some Chinese dialects, tone change is common, and there are complex rules governing it. In contemporary Mandarin, however, it is less common than in other dialects, and there are only a few rules regarding tone change to remember. The first rule governs falling-rising (3rd) tones when they are spoken in sequence:

1. When two falling-rising (3rd) tones occur together, the first falling-rising tone becomes a rising (2nd) tone. The second remains a falling-rising (3rd) tone.

For example, *hen* ("very") and *hao* ("good") are both falling-rising (3rd) tones by themselves, but when spoken together as *hen hao,* the first word changes to a rising (2nd) tone, while the second keeps its original falling-rising (3rd) tone.

2. When three falling-rising tones are spoken one after the other, the first two become rising (2nd) tones, while the third remains a falling-rising tone.

• •

3. When four falling-rising tones occur one after the other, the first three change from falling-rising tones to rising (2nd) tones, while the fourth remains a falling-rising (3rd) tone.

In contemporary Mandarin, tone change is also associated with two specific characters. The first of these is *yi* or "one."

1. *yi* is a high level (1st) tone when it is by itself or at the end of a word.

2. When *yi* comes before a falling (4th) tone, it changes to a rising (2nd) tone, for example, *yi* (2nd) *yue* (4th) ("one month").

3. When *yi* comes before any of the three remaining tones (high, rising, or falling-rising), it changes to a falling (4th) tone.

The second character associated with tone change in contemporary Mandarin is *bu* ("no" or "not").

1. When *bu* stands alone, it is a falling (4th) tone.

• •

2. *bu* changes tone in only one combination. When it comes before another falling (4th) tone, it changes to a rising (2nd) tone.

3. When combined with all the other tones, *bu* remains a falling tone.

Traditional Language Beliefs

Just as the number thirteen is traditionally regarded as unlucky in the West, the Chinese number four, *si*, is seen as ominous, because it is very similar to the pronunciation of the word for "death." For this reason, you may not find a fourth floor in some Chinese-speaking communities. The only difference in this case is that "four," *si*, is pronounced with a falling tone, while the word for "death," *si*, is pronounced with a tone that falls and rises again.

Conversely, the number eight, *ba,* is regarded as lucky, since it shares the same ending sound with the character meaning "to prosper," *fa*.

The number nine, *jiu,* carries a positive meaning as this word sounds exactly like the Chinese

• •

word meaning "long-lasting," *jiu*. These two words are represented in writing by two different characters, but when spoken, the distinction is made only through context.

Color Symbolism

Colors tend to be associated with different meanings in different cultures. It's often useful to be aware of these different connotations.

In Chinese culture, the color red traditionally implies good fortune or good cheer. It is customary to use this color when decorating for such traditional occasions as the celebration of a wedding or a birth. For this reason, brides wear red, babies are clad in red, and red is used most often when decorating for the annual festivals. However, in today's China, many people are adopting more typically Western styles of dress. For instance, many brides are combining Eastern and Western traditions, choosing to wear a white gown to the wedding ceremony, and then changing into a traditional red gown for the wedding banquet.

• •

In the West, the prevalent color seen at a funeral is black, but the main color seen at funerals in China is white, the Chinese traditional color of mourning.

Names and Titles

As in many other Asian cultures, in China the society or group is valued more highly than the individual. Your importance is measured by your value to the group, rather than by those qualities which distinguish you from others.

This can be seen in the way a person is named in Chinese. The most important element of the person's name is thought to be the family of which he or she is a member, and so the family name is spoken first. The given name, which sets the person apart even from others within the same family, is the final element. For example, in the name *Wang Zhuo Hua*, *Wang* is the family name, or surname, and *Zhuo Hua* the given name. Some surnames have a specific meaning: *Wang,* a very common Chinese surname, means "king."

Names and Titles (continued)

• •

The given name is represented by either one or two one-syllable characters. A child's given name is usually chosen very carefully, to represent the parents' hopes for and expectations of the child. In the given name *Zhuo Hua*, *Zhuo* means "outstanding" or "remarkable," while *Hua* can mean "magnificent" or "extravagant."

Westerners are usually referred to by a phonetic representation of their names. Japanese and Korean names are pronounced according to their corresponding forms in Chinese characters.

Children usually take their fathers' family names; on rare occasions the mother's family name may also be used. Most family names are written using single characters. There are a few two-character last names in use: among these, *Situ* and *Ouyoung* are two of the most common.

The Concept of *mian zi* --- "Face"

Language is not an isolated phenomenon, but a vibrant, flexible form of communication loaded with social and cultural information. Chinese culture is structured around such values as honor, loyalty, and respect. In fact, the respect with which a person's community regards him or her can serve as an important part of that person's identity. In Mandarin, this is often referred to as *mian zi,* or "face." Here are some common phrases illustrating this concept:

you mian zi, "to have face," means to be shown respect in a certain social situation. For example, when attending a banquet, those seated near the host at the head of the table can be said "to have face," *you mian zi.*

Similarly, *gei mian zi,* "to give face," means to show someone the respect due him or her. When you attend a formal dinner, the host and hostess might greet you by saying, "Thank you for giving face," which is equivalent to saying, "Thank you for coming."

diu lian," "to lose face," means "to lose dignity." For example, you are thought to lose face if you are the only one of a certain group who is passed over for a promotion or who fails to receive an invitation to a sought-after event.

Compliments

• •

Modesty is seen as an essential virtue in Chinese culture. This humility is shown by some typical responses a Chinese person will give when complimented. For example, a woman who is told *ni zhen piao liang* ("You are really very beautiful") could answer, *na li?* This literally means, "Where is it?" Used in this way, it is the same as saying, "Where do you get that?"

Another common response to a compliment might be, *kua jiang le!* This means something like, "Excessive praise!" and it's used to say, "You're exaggerating," or "You're flattering me." Either of these can be used as a polite, modest response to almost any compliment. Some more Westernized people may also answer simply, *xie xie ni* or "thank you" when complimented, but this is less common.

Chinese Cuisine and Tea

A traditional Chinese saying, "Food is the first necessity of the people," is reflected in the great variety of Chinese food and its importance in traditional celebrations. There are eight schools of cuisine, each associated with a particular geographic region:

• •

Beijing, Guandong, Sichuan, Jiangsu, Zhejiang, Hunan, Anhui, and *Fujian.*

The staple of a Chinese meal is *fan* or cooked rice. In the agricultural south, the *fan* may be rice or rice products. In Northern China, noodles, dumplings, and other staples made from wheat flour are the basis of the daily diet. The meat and / or vegetables that accompany the *fan* are called *cai,* or accompanying dishes.

The custom of drinking tea is also an important part of Chinese culture. The Chinese were the first to discover the tea leaf. A proverb states that it is "better to be deprived of food for three days, than tea for one." When a guest arrives, it is traditional that a cup of tea will be brewed for him or her. The preparation of tea is regarded as an art form; the method of brewing it and the utensils used are very important.

People throughout the country drink tea daily, often in a local tea house, where one may meet informally with friends or associates, or hold a banquet or reception.

The Chinese Zodiac

• •

The Chinese have a system of astrology dating back thousands of years. The Chinese zodiac differs from the Western in that each sign represents an entire year, rather than one month.

According to ancient Chinese legend, Buddha summoned all the animals. He honored those who came by naming a year for them. Thereafter, the characteristics of each animal were given to people born in its year.

The twelve year cycle begins with the Year of the Rat, *shu*; followed in succession by the Year of the Ox, *niu*; Tiger, *hu*; Rabbit, *tu*; Dragon, *long*; Snake, *she*; Horse, *ma*; Goat, *yang*; Monkey, *hou*; Rooster, *ji*; Dog, *gou*; and Boar, *zhu*.

Here is the list of animals associated with each year, along with a list of the qualities traditionally associated with each.

Anyone born during the Year of the **Rat** is expected to be imaginative, charming and generous, with a tendency to be quick-tempered and somewhat critical. Recent Years of the Rat have been 1936, 1948, 1960, 1972, 1984, 1996, and 2008. The next

• •

one will be in 2020. Among famous people born in the year of the Rat are William Shakespeare and George Washington.

The Year of the **Ox** follows. Someone born during an Ox year is both intelligent and perceptive, as well as one who inspires confidence. Napoleon and Vincent Van Gogh were born in the year of the Ox.

A person born in the Year of the **Tiger** is traditionally courageous and considerate of others, as well as stubborn and emotional. Marco Polo and Mary, Queen of Scots were born in the Year of the Tiger.

If a person is born in the Year of the **Rabbit**, he or she will be affectionate and obliging, successful in the business world despite being shy. Some well-known people born in this year were Confucius, Albert Einstein, and Rudolph Nureyev.

A **Dragon** is a perfectionist who is full of vitality and enthusiasm. Pearl Buck, Joan of Arc, and Sigmund Freud were all born in the Year of the Dragon.

• •

Someone born in the Year of the **Snake** is wise and beautiful, with a good sense of humor. Famous Snakes were Charles Darwin, Abraham Lincoln, and Edgar Allan Poe.

If you were born in the Year of the **Horse**, you will be intelligent, hard-working, and very independent. Some famous Horses were Rembrandt, Chopin, and Teddy Roosevelt.

Someone born in the Year of the **Goat** will be charming and artistic, but be relatively uncomfortable in a leadership role. Among famous people born in this year were Michelangelo and Mark Twain.

A person born in the Year of the **Monkey** is clever and witty, with a gift for detail. Famous people born in this year were Julius Caesar, Leonardo da Vinci, and Harry Truman.

A **Rooster** is shrewd and outspoken, as well as extravagant. Rudyard Kipling, Enrico Caruso, and Groucho Marx were all born in this year.

• •

Someone born in the Year of the **Dog** is loyal and honest, although demanding of those around him or her. Famous Dogs were Benjamin Franklin and George Gershwin.

A person born in the Year of the **Boar** is sincere, tolerant, and honest, with an ability to carry out difficult goals. Albert Schweitzer and Ernest Hemingway were born in this year.

Hospitality

During your travels, you may find yourself invited to dinner in a Chinese home. Here are some customs which relate to hospitality and correct behavior as a dinner guest.

It is both appropriate and polite to bring a small gift such as a bottle of wine or a tea set. However, it's best not to bring four of anything, as the number four, *si,* is considered unlucky because it is similar to the word meaning death, *si.* Also, a timepiece of any kind would be inappropriate since the words *song zhong*, meaning "give clock," are very similar to the words meaning "attend someone's funeral."

Hospitality (continued)

● ●

When greeting your host or hostess, you can say *ni hao*, a greeting which means "you (are) good," or "you (are) well." A Chinese "hello," therefore, is a well-wishing hello. *ni hao ma,* or "How are you?" is used by relatives, friends, or acquaintances as an expression of concern, and not as a casual greeting.

As in the West, it's considered rude to immediately begin eating when served. Rather, it's polite to wait until everyone has been seated and all of the dishes have been served. Once this has been done, it's customary for the host or hostess to say, *qing*. This is similar to the American expression, "Please start."

At a more formal dinner party, a toast is frequently offered before the food is served. The person offering the toast could say, *gan bei* or "dry the cup." Another common toast is *zhu ni jian kang,* meaning, "I wish you health."

If you have finished while others are still eating, you should say *qing man yong* ("Please, slowly eat") meaning, "Take your time, enjoy your dinner." After this you can leave the table.

Hospitality (continued)

· ·

When you are leaving the home of your host and hostess, they may say to you, *man zou!* This literally means, "Slowly walk!" and in this situation, it's like saying, "Have a safe trip home!"

Chinese Festivals

Chinese New Year

Chinese festivals are based on the traditional lunar calendar. The Chinese New Year, known as the Spring Festival or *chun jie,* is the most important festival of the year and usually occurs between January 21st and February 19th, according to the Western solar calendar. The entire family is present and a great deal of preparation is involved in cooking special foods which have a symbolic value. Dumplings, *jiao zi,* are considered lucky because they resemble traditional Chinese gold ingots and will be a part of the northern Chinese meal, while a southern household will have a multi-course banquet with more meat served than usual. The New Year celebration ends with the Lantern Festival on the 15th day of the new year. Colorful paper lanterns are lit, some with riddles on them. People eat sweet dumplings made from sticky rice.

Chinese Festivals (continued)
• •

On the eve of the Chinese New Year, the family stays up through the night to watch fireworks which will scare away demons and bad luck. In rural China, or in a traditional household, an elaborate meal will be laid on the family altar table and offered to the family's forbearers accompanied by incense, paper money, and fruit. People will also kowtow to the ancestors for blessing the family throughout the year.

Pure and Bright Day

Another important festival is *qing ming,* or "Pure and Bright Day," which is celebrated around April 5th. Families visit cemeteries to honor their ancestors and beautify their graves. As this festival occurs in spring, it is also a day for sporting contests, kite flying, and other outdoor activities.

Dragon Boat Festival

The festival of *duan wu* is celebrated between late May and early June. The legend connected with this day has to do with the great ancient poet Qu Yuan, who lived more than 2000 years ago in the Kingdom

• •

of Chu in southern China. As legend has it, the poet was deeply patriotic. However, maligned by jealous courtiers, Qu Yuan was banished from Chu. Upon learning that Chu had fallen to a rival army, he threw himself into the Miluo River in present-day Hunan province. The people of Chu rushed to the river to try to save him, but it was too late. They threw bamboo shafts filled with rice as a sacrifice to him, so that the fish would eat the rice and not the poet's body. So on this day, people throw rice dumplings into a river to recreate the sacrifice. It is also customary to eat these dumplings called *zong zi,* which are made from glutinous rice, red beans, or pork and even salted duck egg yolks and wrapped in reed leaves.

Today, the celebration also includes dragon-boat races to commemorate the "people's poet." Dragons are regarded as supernatural creatures and symbols of good luck. The dragon-shaped boats are similar to canoes. Teams then race the "dragons" to mark the festival of *duan wu.*

Chinese Festivals (continued)

• •

Mid-Autumn Day

Mid-Autumn Day, *zhong qiu,* is the most important holiday after the Chinese New Year. It is celebrated on the 15th day of the eighth month on the lunar calendar. In Chinese culture, the full moon symbolizes "completeness, perfection, reunion." On this day, people eat round "moon cakes" and fruits with a round shape, such as watermelons, oranges, or grapefruits. Traditionally, a person exchanges moon cakes with his or her friends, as well as other gifts. The gift of a moon cake has a ritual significance to the Chinese which is similar to the exchange of Christmas gifts in the West.

Proverbs

"The sky is high, the emperor is far away." – *shan gao huang di yuan.* The Chinese routinely include such sayings in their everyday conversation and have done so since ancient times. This proverb means that a powerful figure is far away, and one can relax and enjoy a measure of freedom.

Proverbs (continued)

• •

Many of these sayings are four to eight characters long. Often they contain literary allusions. As such, they may be difficult to understand for the uneducated, and can be nearly incomprehensible to a foreigner.

Many can be traced to Chinese classics and are didactic in nature. They are often called set expressions. The following is simply a small selection of the many examples of Chinese set expressions:

Proverb: *yi ren de dao, ji quan sheng tian.*
"When one man finds the way to success, even his chickens and dogs ascend to heaven."

Meaning: When a man is promoted to a position of authority, all his friends and relatives benefit.

• • • • • • • • • • •

Proverb: *guo he tan shi.*
"Feeling stones while crossing a river."

Meaning: Feeling out the situation as one goes.

• • • • • • • • • • •

Proverb: *gua tian li xia.*
"Never pull on your shoes in a melon patch; never adjust your cap under a plum tree."

Meaning: Don't act suspiciously if you want to avoid being suspected.

Proverbs (continued)

• •

Proverb: *yi bu deng tian.*
"One step, ascend heaven."

Meaning: This is said of someone who has a meteoric rise in fame or fortune.

• • • • • • • • • •

Proverb: *lai er bu wang fei li ye.*
"Come and not go not polite."

Meaning: It is impolite not to reciprocate.

• • • • • • • • • •

Proverb: *sheng bai nai bing jia chang shi.*
"Victories, defeats, are a general's ordinary things."

Meaning: Another victory or defeat doesn't mean much, it's only one part of a whole; par for the course.

• • • • • • • • • •

Proverb: *zuo chi shan kong.*
"Sit, eat, mountain empty."

Meaning: Sit idle and eat, and in time your whole fortune will be used up.

• • • • • • • • • •

Proverb: *yi luan ji shi.*
"Use egg to strike rock."

Meaning: To grossly overestimate one's own strength.

Proverbs (continued)

• •

Proverb: *tu qiong bi xian.*
"Map unrolled, dagger revealed."

Meaning: Someone's real intention is revealed in the end.

• • • • • • • • • • •

Proverb: *Zhang guan Li dai.*
"Zhang's cap on Li's head."

Meaning: To confuse one thing with another.

• • • • • • • • • • •

Proverb: *hu jia hu wei.*
"A fox assumes a tiger's prowess."

Meaning: To bully others by flaunting one's powerful connections.

• • • • • • • • • • •

Proverb: *lu si shei shou.*
"You never know at whose hand a deer will die."

Meaning: There is no way to predict who will prevail in the end.

• •

In Mandarin, there are three ways to ask yes / no questions: by using *ma,* a spoken question word, at the end of the question, or by using a verb / negative form of the verb combination. *ma* is more often used, especially in conversation, as it is perceived as a faster way to pose a question. For example, you can ask either *ni xiang he cha ma*? – meaning, "Would you like to drink tea?" – or *ni xiang bu xiang he cha*? –"You would / wouldn't like to drink tea?" Either form is equally correct. The simplest way, however, is to just raise the tone of your sentence. Usually, this is done to express surprise: "You want to drink tea?"

Currency

Currency in China is called *renminbi,* or the "people's currency," the *yuan* being the standard unit of *renminbi*. Only in recent years has the government allowed *renminbi* to be taken out of the country and exchanged for foreign currency.

Transportation

• •

For most of the Chinese, travel is done on bikes, buses, trains, or on foot, although increasingly more and more people own cars. In fact, China has overtaken the United States as the world's largest automobile market. The government has created a network of highways that will eventually link the major cities. Domestic air travel is also increasingly becoming available. To attract customers airlines often offer steeply discounted airfares.

Communication

Communication systems exist in the major cities and in some less urban areas. All TV channels are operated by the government; local stations as well as radio stations must have official approval. The telephone system is also government owned and operated and continues to expand. Computers, fax machines, electronic mail, and other modern forms of communication are commonplace. Text messaging is far more popular in China than in the United States.

Education

• •

In 1978, China adopted an education policy that mandates compulsory education for nine years. This policy requires students to finish primary school and middle school. Each family is charged a fee per term to send a child to school. Thereafter, students who wish to pursue further education must pass rigorous exams for the high school level and beyond. Entrance to a national university or college requires passing an exam which takes place every July. Due to the exam's difficulty and the harsh weather in that month, students have nick-named it "Black July." Most of the students who complete a higher education are trained as specialists in fields such as engineering and the sciences in order to further China's development.

MANDARIN

*go*Chinese

· ·

Speak & Learn the Pimsleur® Way

Culture Notes

PART TWO

Part Two　　goChinese · Mandarin

TABLE OF CONTENTS

• •

Part Two   *go*Chinese · Mandarin

TABLE OF CONTENTS (continued)
• •

Regional Accents

• •

Mandarin, China's standard spoken language, is taught in schools throughout mainland China and Taiwan. It has become even more widespread through the reach of television. Today virtually all young people on both sides of the Taiwan Strait understand and speak Mandarin, in addition to their native dialects.

As you might expect, the degree of fluency varies. Few people in the South can reproduce the kind of Mandarin heard on television or in films. For instance, when southerners speak Mandarin, they tend to stress every syllable. The "soft sound," also known as the "neutral tone," is often absent from their speech. Whereas Northerners will leave particles and the last syllable of certain compound words unstressed, people from Taiwan or Hong Kong are more likely to give equal stress to each syllable. For example, Northerners will pronounce the word that means "to be acquainted with" as *renshi* (falling and neutral tones), while Southerners will pronounce it *ren sh'*, stressing the last syllable and giving it its full dictionary tonal value. The neutral tone always occurs in the last syllable of a compound word. Stressing it does not usually cause

• •

confusion or misunderstanding, but it does mark the speaker as a Southerner.

Particles

In Chinese, particles, such as *le, de,* and *ne,* perform a number of important functions; for this reason, they are sometimes called "function words." For instance, to indicate that an action has already taken place, you add *le* to the verb: *chi le*, "ate;" *kan le*, "saw." The particle *de* can indicate possession: *wo de shu*, "my book." *ne* as in *ni ne,* means "What about you?" Particles, including these three, are always pronounced with the neutral tone. The word "neutral" is used because their exact tonal value depends on that of the preceding syllable. Whatever tonal value they acquire in natural speech is barely audible. That is why they are also said to be "soft."

• •

Apart from the imperial cuisine associated with the Manchu emperors, in the past Beijing was not particularly known for fine dining. The restaurant scene, however, has changed dramatically in recent years. Now tens of thousands of restaurants featuring a vast array of cooking styles dot the city. Good and inexpensive local food is plentiful, as well as exotic fare from all over the world. As people become more and more affluent, they are increasingly dining out. One of the most famous traditional restaurants in Beijing is *Quanjude*. Its Peking duck is renowned throughout China.

• •

   Chengde is a resort city about 135 miles northeast of Beijing. In 1703 Emperor Kangxi started constructing a summer palace in what was then an obscure provincial town. Eventually the palace grew to the size of Beijing's Summer Palace and the Forbidden City combined. The summer retreat, called *Bishu Shanzhuang,* or Heat-Fleeing Mountain Villa, boasts a vast park. Because their empire was both large and multi-ethnic, the imperial family made a concerted effort to accommodate the Mongolians and other followers of Tibetan and Mongolian Buddhism. To this end they built a group of Lamaist temples to the northwest of the palace. The Qing court not only summered in Chengde, but also received Mongolian and Tibetan leaders and some European diplomats there. Recently the local government has restored many of the palace structures and temples for the sake of tourism. UNESCO has designated the former imperial Summer Palace at Chengde a World Heritage Site.

Alcoholic Beverages

· ·

Among urban and Westernized Chinese, beer is the most popular alcoholic beverage. Despite joint ventures with international wine makers, the production and consumption of wine lag far behind that of beer. Many people, however, prefer Chinese hard liquor to either beer or wine. A formal meal or banquet would not be complete without what the Chinese call *bai jiu,* or white liquor made from grains. Rice wine, served warm, is popular in certain parts of China as well. Almost all liquor is consumed to accompany food.

Although many people have heard of cocktails, they are not common even among Chinese who are reasonably familiar with western ways.

Friends and Family
• •

Foreigners visiting China are most likely to interact with the Chinese in a business setting. After a meeting, guests are often treated to a lavish multicourse meal in a fancy restaurant or hotel. Some tourist agencies also arrange for tourists to spend a day with a Chinese family. Away from tourist hotels and official interpreters, however, spontaneous invitations to one's home are infrequent.

Since most Chinese live in cramped apartments, they are less inclined to invite friends to their home than are Americans. Relatives, of course, are another matter. While three generations living under one roof is becoming increasingly rare, especially in urban areas, close relatives still frequently visit one another.

Teahouses

• •

Teahouses were once ubiquitous in market towns and other urban centers in China. The mainly male clientele went to teahouses not only to quench their thirst, but also to socialize. To attract more patrons, teahouses provided various forms of entertainment such as storytelling and puppet theater. Although tea remains the most popular non-alcoholic beverage today, traditional-style teahouses have virtually disappeared from the Chinese urban landscape.

Women in the Workforce

The percentage of women working outside the home is quite high in China. In cities, virtually all women have jobs. As in the U. S., women dominate certain professions, such as teaching and nursing. There are also many women doctors and scientists. In other important areas, however, they haven't yet achieved parity with men. Women who occupy positions of power are still rare. The burden of restructuring the manufacturing industries in the last twenty years has also fallen more heavily on women, as they are more likely to be laid off than their male counterparts. Older, unskilled women in particular have difficulty finding a job.

Travel in China by Train and Plane

• •

The transportation system in China has seen vast improvements in recent years. The coastal areas are well served by an ever-expanding network of railroads and highways, while all over the country, numerous airports have been built or expanded.

Trains, often packed to capacity, are the traditional people-movers in China. Instead of first or second class, passengers choose hard seat, hard sleeper, soft seat, or soft sleeper. Despite its name, hard seat is in fact not hard, but padded. Since those fares are the cheapest, hard seat is often uncomfortably crowded. By contrast, a sleeper carriage can accommodate only a limited number of people. There are half a dozen bunks in three tiers; sheets, pillows, and blankets are provided. On short distances some trains have soft seats, which cost about the same as hard sleeper. In soft seat, overcrowding and smoking are not permitted. Soft sleeper is the ultimate luxury, with four comfortable bunks in a closed compartment complete with wood paneling, potted plants, lace curtains, and often air-conditioning. Since few Chinese can afford soft sleeper, tickets, which cost twice as much as those for hard sleeper, are easy to obtain.

• •

China has many different types of trains, although there are three main ones: slow, direct express, and special express. Conditions in trains are improving considerably. Faced with stiff competition from airlines and long distance buses, the state-owned rail bureaus have tried to introduce faster and cleaner services, especially to tourist destinations. The most exciting development for lovers of rail travel, however, is China's plan to build the world's largest network of high-speed railways by 2020. The country is already home to the world's only commercial application of the magnetic levitation technology. It is possible to take a Maglev train to downtown Shanghai from its international airport.

Air travel continues to be popular, especially for long-distance travel. There are now frequent flights between major cities.

• •

Shopping is a favorite pastime for many Chinese. Department stores in major cities remain open well after 9:00 PM. Western-style convenience stores have also appeared in big cities; so has warehouse merchandizing. Many of the more popular department stores and supermarkets are joint ventures with international retail giants. Designer brands and labels are available to those who can afford them. By contrast, state-owned stores cater to the tastes and purchasing power of the working class. Street peddlers selling counterfeit goods, fake Prada jackets, Gucci shoes, etc., are popular with local residents and western tourists alike.

• •

Taiwan lies across a narrow strait from southeastern China. It was first settled by aboriginal peoples from Asia. The Chinese began to move to Taiwan in large numbers after the fall of the Ming dynasty in the 1660s. After a humiliating defeat in the Naval Battle of 1895, the Manchu government ceded Taiwan to Japan, which became its colonial master for half a century. After the Second World War, Taiwan reverted to Chinese sovereignty. In 1949 the Nationalist government retreated to Taiwan after losing the civil war with the Communists. Todaythe People's Republic of China is eager to reunite with the island under the "one country, two systems" model. This formula, first proposed to Hong Kong, is meant to assure the Taiwanese that they will be able to maintain their economic and political system after reunification with the mainland.

While official relations across the Taiwan Strait have experienced ups and downs in the last two decades, economic integration is progressing apace. Taiwanese businessmen are eager to exploit their cultural and linguistic ties to the mainland. Today they can be found in all corners of the People's Republic, setting up factories and running hotels and restaurants. Despite the Taiwanese government's misgivings, a number of small and medium-sized companies have shifted their manufacturing operations to the mainland, where land and labor costs are far lower than in Taiwan.

Days and Months

It's easy to remember the days of the week in Chinese. Monday is considered the first day of the week and is called "week-one" – *xingqi yi*. To name the rest of the week, one simply adds the appropriate number to the word *xingqi*: *xingqi er* (Tuesday), *xingqi san* (Wednesday), *xingqi si* (Thursday), *xingqi wu* (Friday), and *xingqi liu* (Saturday). Sunday is called *xingqi tian,* in colloquial Chinese, or *xingqi ri*, in written formal Chinese. *tian* and *ri* both mean "day."

The seven-day week was introduced to China by Christian missionaries who, instead of using *xingqi*, settled on the word *libai*, meaning "worship." The seven days, therefore, were known as *libai yi* (Monday), *libai er* (Tuesday), and so on, with *libai tian* for Sunday. Because of their religious

• •

overtones, the terms fell out of use in the official media, but they have been preserved in spoken Chinese, particularly in the south and in Taiwan. In fact, there the word *libai* is the norm rather than *xingqi*.

Before the introduction of the seven-day week, the Chinese followed the lunar calendar. Each month was divided into three lunar phases of ten days each. The lunar calendar, or *yinli*, was abolished in 1911. However, traditional holidays and festivals are still observed according to the *yinli*.

The names of the months are similarly straightforward. However, one puts the number before, rather than after, the word for "month," *yue*. January is known as the first month, February the second month, and so on. Therefore, the twelve months in Chinese are: *yi yue*, January; *er yue*, February; *san yue*, March; *si yue*, April; *wu yue*, May; *liu yue,* June; *qi yue*, July; *ba yue*, August; *jiu yue*, September; *shi yue*, October; *shi yi yue*, November; and *shi er yue*, December.

• •

Cinema was introduced to China one year after its debut in Paris on December 28, 1895. Ever since, film has been an important form of entertainment for the Chinese, especially those living in cities. Hollywood films dominated the Chinese market in the 1930s and '40s. Then, after the founding of the People's Republic of China in 1949, Hollywood films disappeared from the scene. Since the 1990s, when the Chinese government reversed its policy, American blockbusters such as *Forrest Gump* and *Titanic* have drawn large crowds wherever they were shown in China. On the whole, however, audiences are dwin-dling. To attract more customers, Chinese movie theaters have started to convert to American-style multiplexes. Most people, however, watch films at home on pirated VCDs and DVDs, which can be found on every street corner in Chinese cities.

Popular Entertainment

As movie audiences dwindle, other forms of entertainment have taken hold. Karaoke, for instance, has become wildly popular with both young and old at banquets, in bars, or at family

• •

gatherings. Guests are often invited to join in the fun. At times like these it's best to be a good sport and play along, even if you can't hold a tune. Good-natured ribbing and hamming are part of the merriment.

Mahjong, traditionally a game for men and women of leisure, has also regained its popularity after being banned for decades. Small fortunes are won or lost at the mahjong table. Quartets of men or women often play late into the night amidst clouds of cigarette smoke. Card games are also eagerly arranged and anticipated at family reunions and parties.

Beijing Opera

Beijing opera, or literally Beijing drama, is more than just opera. It combines vocal and instrumental music, dance, mime, acrobatics, and occasionally even magic. Props and scenery are minimal: except for a table and a couple of chairs, the stage is bare. Actors specialize in one of four types of roles: the *sheng*, *dan*, *jing*, or *chou*. The *sheng* are the leading male roles. They portray characters like scholars,

• •

officials, and warriors. The *dan* are the female roles.
Traditionally, they were played by men; today,
however, only a few female impersonators are left.
The *jing* are the painted-face roles. These usually
include martial or heroic characters and supernatural
beings. The *chou* are essentially comic roles. The
actors wear clown make-up – often a small white
triangle between the eyes and across the nose. The
libretti of Beijing opera are adapted from classical
Chinese literature and are well known to those who
regularly attend the performances. The language,
however, is archaic and difficult to understand.
For this reason, lyrics are sometimes projected on
top of the proscenium arch or on one side of the
stage. Reportedly, opera star Beverly Sills attended
a performance of Beijing opera during a visit to
China and subsequently decided to introduce super-
titles at the New York City Opera. Although most
performances of Beijing opera take place in modern
theaters, some ornate, traditional courtyard theaters
have been renovated for tourists.

• •

In the days when the state dominated all facets of the economy, only a small portion of the population, factory directors, party secretaries, and so on, took business trips. The state paid for all their expenses. Today, with a booming private economic sector, China is seeing more and more people criss-crossing the country seeking business opportunities or cementing business ties.

The sight of businessmen in crisp suits and shiny leather shoes boarding trains and planes contrasts starkly with the scene at bus terminals and train stations. There, hordes of peasants from China's inland provinces descend upon the coastal cities. For lack of other accommodations, many remain in the depots. Arriving by the thousands every day, these migrants are fleeing rural poverty and looking for better jobs.

Coffee

Although tea is by far the most popular beverage in China, coffee has made inroads, particularly in big cities.

Coffee (continued)

• •

In the 1920s and '30s, coffee houses in western enclaves in Shanghai and Tianjin were favorite hangouts for writers and students. During the Cultural Revolution (1966-1976), coffee houses, along with western restaurants, virtually disappeared. In recent years, however, American franchises such as Starbucks, called *xingbake* in Chinese, have opened all over China.

Parts of Yunnan province and Hainan Island in southern China are ideal for growing coffee. Nevertheless, to most Chinese in small cities and rural areas, coffee remains a bitter, exotic drink.

Holidays and Leisure Time

In recent years China reduced the six-day work week to five. In addition, employees get at least several days off for each major holiday: the Chinese New Year (late January or February), May Day or Labor Day (May 1st), and National Day (October 1st). These, however, are presently the only paid vacations. Thus on average, Chinese people, at least those who live in urban areas, have from two to three weeks of vacation. Because everyone goes

• •

on vacation at the same time, tourist destinations are jam-packed. Those who crave peace and quiet would do well to avoid traveling around these major holidays.

The increase in leisure time is having a far-reaching impact on China's economy and society, creating financial windfalls for restaurants, amusement parks, hotels, and towns with picturesque waterways or pagodas. Unlike Americans, the Chinese are far less likely to take part in outdoor sports such as skiing or scuba diving when they go on vacation.

Chinese Pastries

Mung bean cakes are small, bite-size pastries made from mung beans; they are especially popular in the south and in Taiwan. Moon cakes are another favorite; they contain various fillings such as red bean paste, lotus seeds, ham, and salted yolks of ducks' eggs. During the Mid-Autumn Festival (August 15th on the lunar calendar, usually sometime in September in the western calendar), the Chinese eat moon cakes in celebration of the full moon.

Chinese Pastries (continued)

● ●

Elaborately packaged moon cakes are frequently exchanged as gifts. Many restaurants derive a substantial part of their annual profits from the Mid-Autumn Festival. Mung bean cakes and moon cakes are frequently served with tea. Desserts are not normally part of a meal in China; they are served only as part of a formal banquet.

Modesty and Politeness

When the Chinese invite friends over for dinner, the host almost always begins a meal with the apology, "There's nothing to eat" – despite the fact that he or she has probably gone all out and prepared a feast. Guests then express unease over the abundance of food on the table and the host's extravagance. This exchange is a social ritual for most Chinese, as Chinese culture highly values modesty. Once the meal begins, the host heaps food on the plates in front of the guests, while the guests exercise restraint. If a guest does not care for a particular dish, it is best to leave it discretely on the plate. This is also a good way to politely discourage overzealous hosts from continuously offering more.

Modesty and Politeness (continued)

The high value placed on modesty also explains why Chinese will deflect a compliment rather than accepting it graciously. For example, when Chinese people receive a compliment, instead of *xiexie*, or "thank you," they say *nali nali*, literally, "Where? Where?" meaning, "There's nothing anywhere worthy of praise." A suitably embarrassed expression accompanies the saying to further show one's modesty. When they accept an offer of help or receive a gift, again, rather than "thank you," the Chinese say *bu hao yi si*, meaning, "This is embarrassing" or "I feel embarrassed [for having imposed on you]."

Like all languages, Chinese has a number of frequently-used formulaic expressions and responses. When an important guest or a customer arrives, Chinese people say *huan ying guang lin*, literally, "Welcome your glorious presence or patronage." When a friend departs on a trip, it is customary to say *yi lu shun feng*, or "May the wind be with you."

• •

Hangzhou lies about 119 miles south of China's largest city, Shanghai. When the Shanghai-Hangzhou Inter-City Railway opens in 2010, travel time will be cut down to 38 minutes. Tourism is an important part of Hangzhou's economy. The city is famous for its picturesque West Lake, which is surrounded by lush hills and has long been eulogized by Chinese poets. Many of the sights around the lake have literary associations. These sights include the Leifeng Pagoda, which collapsed in the 1920s and has since been reconstructed; the causeway; and the stone bridge, especially beautiful when snow-covered in winter. Besides West Lake, Hangzhou is also known for several important Buddhist temples. The villages surrounding Hangzhou produce some of the best tea in China.

Combating the Summer Heat

Summer, which extends from mid-June to the end of September, can be unbearably hot and humid in some parts of China. Before the advent of modern air-conditioning, the Chinese resorted to other methods to stay cool. One inexpensive way was using a fan. Scholars and intellectuals preferred

• •

folding, paper fans. Light in weight and easy to carry around, these folding fans were often works of art as well as highly functional objects. In fact, fan paintings were prized possessions among Chinese men of letters. Women's fans were oval-shaped and made of paper, silk, or feathers. They were often painted as well. Banana trees and legendary beauties were favorite subjects. Today air conditioners are becoming more and more common, yet many Chinese still find fans indispensable.

Moreover, not everyone can afford an air conditioner. Chinese who live in crowded, poorly ventilated old quarters sit under shady trees, playing cards or chatting with their neighbors, trying to catch the cool evening breezes as the sun sets. In addition, all Chinese enjoy popular summer drinks such as ice cold mung bean soup. Those lucky enough to live near the coast take to the beaches in droves. Swimming pools and water parks with various rides are also popular destinations, especially for families with children.

Forms of Address

• •

Unlike Americans, most Chinese are not on a first-name basis with many other people. Personal names alone are rarely used. (In the U.S. they are called "first names," but remember that in China, the family name is spoken first.) It's considered impolite to address one's superior by his or her personal name. The usual practice is to use the family name plus his or her official position or professional title, for example, Principal Tian, Manager Liu, etc. Similarly, the personal pronoun *ni* ("you") is best avoided when talking to one's superior; the more formal *nin* is preferred. Depending on their respective ages, co-workers commonly address each other by adding either *lao* (meaning "old") or *xiao* (meaning "young") to the family name. Personal names are reserved for intimate friends and family members. However, even younger siblings are discouraged from using their older brothers' and sisters' personal names. Instead they say *gege* ("elder brother") or *jiejie* ("elder sister"). In other words, hierarchy and the nature of the relationship play an important role in determining how one refers to or addresses someone else. Also, as in the U.S., it's a good idea to avoid using the third person singular pronoun *ta* ("he" or "she") if the person in question is present.

Travel Outside China

• •

   After 1949, when the Communist Party came into power, China became closed to the rest of the world. For nearly forty years it was almost impossible for ordinary citizens to leave the country. Furthermore, except for state guests, few foreign visitors were allowed into China. Starting in the 1990s, Chinese began to travel abroad as tourists, reflecting the new official "open-door" policy and the increasing prosperity of ordinary Chinese. Popular destinations now include South Korea and Southeast Asian countries such as Singapore, Malaysia, and Thailand. With their recent economic downturn, these countries eagerly welcome Chinese tourists. Japan, New Zealand, Australia, and the European Union are now also granting visas to Chinese tourists.

   Unit recently, Chinese wishing to go abroad had to participate in package tours. It is still very difficult to travel overseas as an individual, although less so than in the past. Likewise, obtaining a passport is also becoming more "hassle-free."

The "Three Links"

● ●

After the Civil War between the Communists and the Nationalists, communications between the Chinese mainland and Taiwan were broken off. As tension mounted across the Taiwan Strait, the two sides exchanged daily barrages of cannon fire. These have ceased. In order to pressure Taiwan into closer integration with mainland China, the Chinese government gave high priority to the renewal of three ties: (1) the resumption of commerce; (2) the exchange of mail, both business and personal; and (3) the establishment of direct connections by air and sea, for both goods and people. Fearing the inexorable pull of these so-called "three links," but also wanting to avoid conflict, the Taiwanese government reacted with its own "Three No" policy: "no" to reunification, "no" to complete independence, "no" to confrontation. Despite the mainland's call for direct navigational links, traffic across the narrow Taiwan Strait still had to be routed through a destination – often Hong Kong or Macau until 2008. Then, acknowledging the increasing economic ties between the two sides of the Taiwan Strait, a newly elected Taiwanese government resumed the direct three links with mainland China.

Personal Questions

• •

Westerners who go to China are often asked about their age, salary, or marital status. Much of China is still predominantly rural in form and mentality, and notions of privacy differ from those in the West. Raised in a culture that venerates old age, the Chinese consider asking how old someone is a perfectly innocuous question. And for decades, everyone in China had more or less the same income. Therefore, the amount of money an acquaintance made was usually not a big secret. Even today, asking about salary is not a breach of etiquette, and can even be polite, indicating an interest in you and your financial well-being. Finally, if a Chinese shows interest in a Westerner's marital status, it is because family is important to the Chinese. Like one's salary, it is also a good topic for conversation. Westerners should not take offense at any of these questions. Rather, anyone who is not comfortable answering them directly can simply deflect them with a general or vague reply.

On the other hand, Chinese people are apt to find Americans' openness to discussing inner turmoil rather puzzling. There is less willingness among the Chinese to talk about issues of depression and other mental health problems.

However, as China becomes more urbanized and commercialized, and the gap in income levels becomes wider, western notions of privacy are beginning to seep into Chinese society. It remains to be seen whether advertising will make the Chinese as youth-obsessed as Americans, but newspaper advice columns are already exhorting readers to refrain from asking women about their ages. *yinsi* (privacy) is being gradually assimilated into everyday vocabulary.

China's One-Child Policy

China has had an official one-child policy since 1979. The policy may seem Draconian to Westerners, but it was deemed necessary by the Chinese government. A fifth of the people in the world live in China. However, only 15 to 20% of the country's land is suitable for agriculture. To ensure sustainable growth, the Chinese government began to enforce population control in earnest in the late 1970s. Exceptions are made in cases of remarriages where one spouse does not have a biological child. Couples whose first child is physically or mentally handicapped are also allowed to have a second child.

• •

Minorities are exempted from the one-child policy as well.

For the most part, family planning has taken hold in the cities. For example, Shanghai and Beijing have achieved zero, or even negative, population growth. Most Chinese people, however, live in rural areas. Implementing the one-child policy in China's vast hinterland has been far more challenging. The increasing mobility of the population also makes it difficult for the government to catch violators of the one-child policy. Those who are caught are subject to penalties that range from fines to the child's being ineligible for free education. The one-child policy has achieved its goal to lower population growth. However, demographers, economists, and sociologists have expressed concerns about the negative consequences of the policy such as a rapidly aging population and the gender imbalance because of society's preference for boys.

The Phone System

• •

Twenty years ago, even in big cities, it was a rare Chinese family that had a telephone. Most people relied on public pay phones. Today practically every adult in China's urban centers owns a cell phone. In fact, China is the largest market for cell phones in the world. Pay phones can be found on almost every street corner. Most of them accept cards only; coin-operated phones are rare.

Paradoxically, because China's phone system was until recently so inadequate, even non-existent in rural areas, the country has been able to leapfrog the old analog technology and employ the latest digital technology that western telecommunications companies have to offer. Today Motorola, Ericsson, Nokia, and Bell-Alcatel all have joint ventures in China.

Banks

• •

The Big Four of China's state-owned banks are Bank of China, Agricultural Bank of China, Industrial and Commercial Bank of China (ICBC), and Construction Bank of China. In addition, many provinces and municipalities have established their own banks; and major international banks have opened branches in China as well. Until recently, foreign banks were required to limit their business solely to foreign currency transactions. However, with China's formal acceptance into the World Trade Organization, foreign banks will increasingly be allowed to conduct business in the local currency, *renminbi*, thus creating competition for the more inefficient state-owned banks.

Nevertheless, Chinese banks have made great strides on the technological front. Computers have replaced abacuses, and ATMs are cropping up everywhere in big cities. A few years ago, Chinese ATMs accepted only local cards. Today, foreign tourists can access their accounts from almost any ATM in China.

• •

The Chinese refer to their country as *zhongguo*, which literally means the Middle or Central Country. In ancient times *zhongguo* referred to the various Chinese states in the central plains in northern China. The word was invented to distinguish the original, ethnic Chinese states from the territories outside Chinese civilization.

Before the twentieth century, the country was named after the reigning dynasty. Therefore, from 1644 to 1911, when China was under Manchu or Qing rule, the country was known as the Great Qing Empire. After the Qing dynasty was over-thrown in 1911, Chinese nationalists called the new republic *zhonghua minguo* (Republic of China) – *zhong guo* for short. When the Communists came to power in 1949, the country was renamed *zhonghua renmin gongheguo* (People's Republic of China). To this day, however, the short version remains *zhongguo*.

Measurements

• •

Like most other countries, China now uses the metric system. Traditional measurements have largely become a thing of the past. One exception is weights. For example, people still ask for a *jin* (half a kilogram, or about a pound) of spinach in a grocery store, or two *liang* (two hundred grams, or about seven ounces) of wonton in a restaurant. In rural areas peasants cling to tradition and measure distance in *li* (half a kilometer, or about a third of a mile). However, only the metric system is officially recognized.

Temperatures are measured on the Celsius scale. Shoe sizes follow the continental European system. Clothing sizes vary. Most follow the European system. Those bearing American brand names, whether or not they are authentic, are often labeled Small, Medium, Large, and Extra Large. These do not necessarily correspond to American sizes, however; an article of clothing marked "Extra Large" in China may be closer to a Medium in the U.S.

Chinese Students Abroad

● ●

In its heyday during the Tang dynasty (618-907), China was a magnet for students from neighboring countries, particularly Japan and Korea. Many took the perilous journey by land or sea to the Tang capital, Chang'an, to study Buddhism, government, and the Chinese language. At the same time, a handful of brave Buddhist priests from China went on an arduous trek to India in search of Buddhist scriptures. However, the Chinese did not begin to study abroad in any significant numbers until the late nineteenth and early twentieth centuries.

After a series of disastrous confrontations with the West and with Japan, the Chinese realized how far they had fallen behind and began for the first time to send students abroad en masse. Because of its geographic proximity and its early start in modernization, Japan became the most popular destination for Chinese students, reversing the historic traffic between the two countries. However, as relations between China and Japan deteriorated in the 1920s and '30s, Chinese headed instead to European and American universities. Then came the Communist Party's rise to power and the Korean War. As a result, during the 1950s and early '60s, the former Soviet Union and Eastern Europe replaced the West as the training ground for Chinese scientists and engineers.

In the ensuing two decades, China isolated itself from the rest of the world. But, in the 1980s, China's brightest and most ambitious were again able to leave the country. This time America was the overwhelming destination of choice. Chinese students now make up one of the largest groups of international students at America's universities, particularly in science and engineering programs. At some of America's best universities, after English, Chinese is the language most commonly heard in the research labs. Many of the key figures in twentieth-century Chinese history studied abroad. Their experiences in Japan, Europe, the former Soviet Union, and America helped to shape every aspect of Chinese society. Chinese students with a foreign education are one of China's most important assets in its quest for modernization.

Medical Care

• •

Like many other things in China, the health care system is also in flux. Previously, health care was the responsibility of individual companies and / or communes, and nearly everyone had universal medical care. Large companies often had their own hospitals for their workers and in rural areas money was set aside by local communes to provide health care. With the economic reforms and the push of the 1980s toward capitalism, the communes were dissolved and hospitals were severed from their companies. Local governments became responsible for the wellbeing of their citizens, which meant there was a lack of resources and funds in poorer areas. In the cities, most residents can now buy into a government run insurance program; however, the reimbursement rates are often very low and most care must be paid for upfront by the patient, the costs of which are often more than the patient makes in a year. These high out-of-pocket expenses often lead many people to stay at home and avoid hospitals and doctors.

The Chinese government has announced a plan to spend over $100 billion between 2010-2020 to overhaul the country's health care system, with an eventual goal of all citizens having more affordable

• •

access to basic medical services. China was once famous for its "barefoot doctors," who served in rural areas. The itinerant doctors were often peasants themselves and often had a rudimentary, but highly practical knowledge of medicine. Part of the government's plan will support programs to offer more training for these remaining doctors as well as incentives, such as tuition reimbursements, to bring more university-trained doctors to rural areas.

Traditional Chinese Medicine

Most people in China swear by traditional Chinese medicine. In the West, the Chinese art of healing is also attracting believers. However, in the first two decades of the twentieth century, Chinese medicine was under attack by intellectuals educated in America and Europe. Along with imperial rule and foot-binding, Chinese medicine was dismissed as part of an outdated, moribund tradition, or even worse, as spurious science. After the founding of the People's Republic of China in 1949, traditional Chinese medicine regained respectability. Specialized colleges were established to train practitioners of Chinese medicine. Today, most

Traditional Chinese Medicine (continued)
• •

Chinese doctors of traditional medicine are schooled in western medicine as well, and they routinely use modern diagnostic tools such as X-rays and MRIs, along with more traditional means.

What primarily sets traditional Chinese medicine apart from its western counterpart is its holistic nature. Rather than treating symptoms, Chinese medicine aims at redressing the imbalance of positive and negative energies. This view of the workings of the human body stems from Chinese cosmology, which sees the universe in dualistic, counteracting terms. In addition to herbs and minerals, acupuncture, massage, and diet are frequently used. "Moxibustion" is another common therapy. This involves the application of *moxa*, a substance obtained from the mugwort herb, either with acupuncture needles or by being burnt on the patient's skin. All these tools make up the therapeutic repertoire of the traditional Chinese physician.

E-mail and Internet Cafés
● ●

Internet cafés have become permanent fixtures of the urban landscape. Public libraries and large bookstores are also good places to get online. Meanwhile, computer ownership is increasing by leaps and bounds. Each year tens of millions of Chinese add computers to the increasingly long list of electronic equipment they own. Cable companies in major cities already offer broadband services.

There is a regional and socioeconomic imbalance in Internet access, reflecting the larger overall disparity in development between the more progressive coastal provinces in the east and the more traditional inland provinces in the west. Because of its capital-intensive nature, the new technology also attracts the young and the affluent of Chinese society. In a country where the government controls the media, the Internet provides an alternative venue for the young and the opinionated to sound off. Internet chat rooms have become an important barometer of the mood of an increasingly influential sector of Chinese society. The government, however, is vigilant in suppressing what it considers subversive views, and must walk a tightrope between nurturing the nascent technology and maintaining political stability.

• •

The largest city in China, Shanghai is a thriving metropolis. Situated at the mouth of the Yangtze River in the middle of China's east coast, Shanghai's location gives the city an unbeatable competitive advantage. On one hand, it reaches along China's longest river into the vast hinterland to the west. On the other hand, it is nearly equidistant from all the major cities in northeast Asia. Beijing, Tokyo, Osaka, Seoul, Hong Kong, and Taipei, are all about two hours away by air.

Until the mid-nineteenth century, Shanghai was a sleepy county seat. Once opened to the West, Shanghai was transformed into a world-class metropolis within decades. By the 1920s it had become China's economic, financial, and cultural center. At the same time it had also acquired a reputation for being one of the most iniquitous places on earth. After 1949 the Chinese government closed down brothels and opium dens; it turned Shanghai into an industrial city, thus stripping it of its dominance in trade, finance, and culture. With the new policy of reform and re-opening up to the West, Shanghai began to experience a renaissance in the 1990s. Today Shanghai is sizzling once again, attracting the

● ●

brightest and the most adventurous from China and from other parts of the world.

The Postal System

The Chinese postal system offers more services than its American counterpart. For instance, most newspapers are delivered by mail. Also, in the days when private phones were few and far between, telephones in the post office provided one of the few options for making domestic and international long-distance calls. Even today the bigger branch offices contain phone booths. However, fewer people are lining up to use them, as phone cards and private phones become more and more common. A relatively new service that is gaining in popularity is postal savings, which offers a convenient alternative to traditional banks. Consumers can now open a savings account at any major post office.

• •

wo zuo di tie qu wo de peng you nar chi wan fan.

A salient feature of Chinese word order is the observance of the chronological principle. Note the example in the title, which means: "I'm going to take the subway to go to my friend's place to have dinner." In English, you could also say: "I'm going to my friend's place by subway to have dinner," or even "I'm going by subway to have dinner at my friend's place." Not so in Chinese. In Chinese, the word order is determined by the sequence of actions: You must get on the subway before you can go to your friend's place. You have to go to the place before you can have dinner there. Similarly, to say that you're going to pick up a friend at the airport, you must literally say, "I'm going to drive my car to go to the airport to pick up my friend." Saying, "I'm going to pick up my friend at the airport" is not possible in Chinese. Another example is the English sentence, "My son is studying at Boston University." Because you have to be *at* the university *before* you can study there, Chinese says literally, "My son at Boston University is studying." Here again the chronological principle is at work.

Chinese Word Order (continued)

• •

Another factor affecting word order in Chinese is "topicalization." When someone or something has already been mentioned, or is the focus or topic of a discussion, then that thing or person must be stated first. For instance, if a Chinese person were asked, "Where did all the moon cakes go?" he or she might answer, "The moon cakes, I finished them all," rather than saying, "I finished all the moon cakes."

Sports and Board Games

For many years table tennis was perhaps the most popular sport in China. The reason is simple: it doesn't require expensive equipment or much space. Amateur teams were established all over the country, and China dominated the sport in international competitions for decades.

Bowling was introduced to China in the late 1980s. It quickly replaced table tennis in popularity. However, so many bowling alleys were built that today many stand empty.

• •

The most popular spectator sport in China is soccer. All over the country, soccer clubs have loyal followings. Fans often travel to different parts of the country to follow the matches of local clubs against their competitors.

Traditional sports such as shadow boxing, or *taijiquan*, are popular with women and the elderly. Every morning tens of thousands of retirees practice it in parks and on street corners to taped music. In addition to *taijiquan*, other Chinese martial arts are also popular. But because they are so intense, martial arts require years of training under experienced masters. There are many different styles and schools of martial arts, which are often rivals. Perhaps the most famous school of martial arts is the Shaolin Temple in the Henan province. It was an important center of Chinese *chan* Buddhism, better known in the U.S. by the Japanese pronunciation, *zen* Buddhism. Shaolin is also famous for having produced generations of martial monks. Today Shaolin's reputation is built primarily on its martial arts school. Its history as the place where Bodhidharma, the founder of *chan* Buddhism, achieved enlightenment is much less well known.

Sports and Board Games (continued)

• •

Besides *taijiquan* and martial arts, the Chinese also enjoy more cerebral sports such as Chinese chess and the board game *weiqi*, better known in the West by its Japanese name, *go*. Chinese chess is said to descend from the same ancestor as international chess. All over China, in villages and cities, young and old play Chinese chess.

The esoteric *weiqi* has a more exalted status. Traditionally, it was one of the four requisite accomplishments for the well-educated man of leisure – the other three being music, calligraphy, and painting. *weiqi* still has an elitist image today. Its name means, "game of encirclement." Played with 180 white stones and 181 black stones on a grid consisting of 19 horizontal and 19 vertical lines, the game appears deceptively simple. Its complexity rises from the immense number of possible board positions. Every year corporations in Japan, China, and Korea sponsor tournaments attracting the best professional players from these three countries.

• • • • • • • • • • • • • • • • • • •

Finding one's way around large Chinese cities is a relatively straightforward affair. Many cities, especially provincial capitals, were laid out in a grid pattern. Street names are often written in both Chinese characters and *pinyin* (a transcription into Roman letters). Buses are plentiful, but they can be uncomfortably crowded; and for foreigners who don't know the local language, it can be difficult to know where to get off.

Several cities, such as Beijing, Tianjin, Shanghai, and Guangzhou, boast subways, and still others have plans to build them.

For city-dwellers who are in a hurry or do not wish to fight for standing room in a crowded bus, taxis, or *chuzu qiche,* have become a welcome alternative. "To take a taxi" in Mandarin is *zuo chuzu qiche*, or simply *zuo chuzu*. In recent years, another term has come into popular usage: *da di*, which comes from Cantonese. *di* is a short form of the Cantonese word for "taxi." Although taxis are more expensive than buses, they are still affordable for the average citizen.

• •

Several models of taxis predominate, depending on the city. Because of regional protectionism, locally made cars are often favored over models made in other parts of the country. For this reason, nearly all the taxis in Shanghai are Volkswagens made by a Shanghai-based joint venture with the German carmaker. In Tianjin the city was overrun with small taxis called *xiali* made locally with Japanese parts. The municipal government of Shanghai banned *xiali* from the city several years ago, claiming that they were big polluters and incongruous with the image of the city as a world-class metropolis. In any taxi, it's a good idea to ask for a receipt; this will help to ensure that you are charged a fair rate.

Rickshaws, once ubiquitous in China, disappeared decades ago and can be seen only in films or tourist spots in a few cities.

• •

   Parks in the English sense of the word did not exist in imperial China. Emperors had their hunting preserves, scholar-officials their private gardens. Both had long traditions in China, and both were off limits to intruders (or commoners). For ordinary urban dwellers in a predominantly rural society, temple grounds and open-air markets provided the main public spaces. Western-style parks were first introduced to urban Chinese in the late nineteenth century in semi-colonial cities such as Shanghai and Tianjin. The first park in Shanghai, laid down by the British, was known as the Public Park. Its front gate reputedly featured a placard forbidding dogs and Chinese from entry. The authenticity of this legend is disputed, but it has become part of the nationalistic Chinese lore. After the Republican revolution in the early twentieth century, former imperial playgrounds were opened to the public. Many of the famous parks in Beijing, such as the Summer Palace Park and Beihai Park, had imperial beginnings.

Currency

• •

In the old days of chronic shortages, western hard currencies were highly coveted by the Chinese. Those lucky enough to have foreign currency remittances from overseas could shop in special stores. As a result, black markets dealing in foreign currency exchange thrived. Today, China is one of the biggest trading nations in the world with a huge foreign exchange reserve. The government has therefore somewhat relaxed its control on currency exchange.

Foreign tourists, of course, have no trouble exchanging money in China. Big tourist hotels, airports, major bank branches, upscale department stores – all provide currency exchange services. Chinese wishing to travel abroad can also obtain foreign currency up to an amount set by the government at local banks. However, the Chinese currency, *renminbi*, (literally, "people's money,") is still not fully convertible, which to a certain extent insulates the Chinese economy from the rest of the world. The government has plans to make the *renminbi* fully convertible, but there is no formal official timetable.

• •

Feng shui, the traditional art of auspicious siting, has become a fad in the West in recent years. Even some Fortune 500 companies have hired feng shui masters to improve the circulation of positive energy. Ironically, in China the practice largely disappeared after the Communists came into power, and feng shui was dismissed as feudal superstition. Since then it has made a comeback, especially in southeastern China. Private business owners frequently consult with feng shui experts in order to site their factories and homes in the most auspicious locations and thereby improve their balance sheets.

Feng shui is an amalgam of ancient Chinese beliefs. The aim of feng shui is to bring various water bodies and land configurations into complete harmony so as to direct the flow of *qi*, or vital energy. Benefits of good feng shui encompass health and longevity, prosperity, fecundity, and general happiness, and they extend to one's descendents. According to the principles of feng shui, an ill-chosen site for a grave, for instance, will adversely affect the well-being of one's children.

Part Two

Qingdao

• •

Qingdao, also known as Tsingtao, sits on a peninsula in Northern China. The city is known for its abundant local seafood and for its previous incarnation as a German colony. In the minds of most Chinese, and frequent patrons of Chinese restaurants in the West, the name of the city is synonymous with its eponymous beer. The local brewery is the largest domestic producer of beer in China and part of the city's German legacy. In addition to the light thirst-quencher, Qingdao's beaches, fresh air, clean streets, and German architecture make the city one of the most popular tourist destinations in China.

• •

Except for a brief period of time when the Nationalist Party was in power, Beijing, formerly known in the West as Peking, has been the capital of China since the Yuan Dynasty (1206-1368). In 1928 the Nationalist government moved the capital to Nanjing and renamed Beijing "Beiping." When the Chinese Communist Party drove the Nationalists to Taiwan in 1949, Beijing resumed both its original name and its status as the capital of China. Beijing, literally "Northern Capital," is the political and cultural center of a highly centralized country. While the massive wall surrounding the city was destroyed in the 1950s, the vast former imperial palace complex, known as the Forbidden City, can still be visited. It now houses the Palace Museum. Other tourist attractions include the Great Wall, which lies outside the city, the Summer Palace, and the Temple of Heaven.

• •

Chinese travelers are abandoning boat travel en masse in favor of other means of transportation. China's network of highways is expanding, and air travel is increasingly affordable. Several long-standing services, for instance those from Shanghai to Ningbo, a seaport to the south, were recently discontinued. Cruise ships, however, are another matter.

Boat travel may be declining, but Chinese water-ways are getting busier every year. The government is dredging rivers and widening canals in hopes of increasing freight shipping. In fact, one of the benefits of the controversial Three Gorges dam project is the improvement of the navigability of the upper Yangtze River. With the creation of a huge reservoir, there is a more constant water level and wider shipping lanes.

Nanjing

• •

   Nanjing, in southeastern China, is one of the
more attractive cities in the country. It was the
capital of China during the Six Dynasty period, from
222-589. During the Ming and Qing Dynasties,
from the fourteenth to the nineteenth centuries, the
city was an important economic and cultural center.
The old pleasure quarter along the Qinhuai Creek
was famous throughout China, as was the Confucian
Temple. Both have been restored for the benefit of
tourists. In addition, Nanjing boasts the longest city
wall in the world, as well as numerous other historic
sites. Nanjing is also known for its steamy summer
weather. Together with Wuhan and Chongqing,
Nanjing is one of the so-called "Three Furnaces" on
the Yangtze River.

• •

Tianjin, 75 miles from Beijing, is the capital's gateway to the sea. It is also the largest industrial center in northern China. It was one of the five cities opened to foreign trade in the nineteenth century by the Qing government. Western powers were able to carve out enclaves in the city, and this history is reflected in its architecture. Because of its proximity to Beijing, however, Tianjin often finds itself playing second fiddle to its powerful neighbor.

English in China

English is a highly marketable skill in present-day China. Proficiency in English can lead to a high-paying job with an international company or to a chance to study abroad. Although Chinese students begin learning English as early as elementary or middle school, teachers and textbooks emphasize grammar over communication. Therefore, while many educated Chinese can read English, few can speak it fluently. For this reason many people attend special English language schools or classes in their spare time. In fact, many government institutions and offices pay employees to take English classes during work hours. English language schools abound, as do textbooks and instructional tapes. English teachers are in great demand, and it is not unusual for tourists to be approached by young people wishing to hone their conversational skills.

MANDARIN

*go*Chinese

Speak & Learn the Pimsleur® Way

Culture Notes

PART THREE

Part Three   *go*Chinese · Mandarin

TABLE OF CONTENTS

• •

TABLE OF CONTENTS (continued)

• •

China's Weather

● ●

    Because of its vast size, China's weather varies a great deal from north to south, east to west. From the sub-arctic in the northeast to the subtropical in parts of Yunnan province in the southwest, China covers several climate zones. The three northeastern provinces – Heilongjiang, Jilin, and Liaoning – are bitterly cold in the winter, with temperatures often dipping to minus forty degrees Fahrenheit. China's population of 1.2 billion (five times that of the United States) is largely centered in the eastern part of the country. The terrain in the west consists largely of mountains and deserts. Although China boasts some of the world's longest rivers, only land in the east is fertile enough to support agriculture. The nation's capital, Beijing, receives a fair amount of snow, although heavy storms and blizzards are rare. To escape the winter weather, tourists flock to the warm, sandy beaches of Hainan Island in the South China Sea. Xishuangbanna in Yunnan is another popular winter destination for those who wish to escape the cold. Summer is the rainiest season in China. From mid-June to mid-July much of the lower Yangtze River valley is shrouded in rain. Sea resorts like Qingdao and Beidaihe in the north, and mountainous regions like Putuoshan and Lushan in the south, provide relief from the stifling heat and humidity.

• •

Spring and autumn are probably the best times to visit China: throughout much of the country, the skies are clear, with daytime temperatures hovering between sixty and eighty degrees Fahrenheit. However, Beijing, which used to be famous for its clear, azure-blue, autumnal skies, now suffers from smog and air pollution. In addition, every spring the winds from the Gobi desert bring heavy sandstorms from the north. Although the government has mounted a massive campaign to reforest northern and northwestern China, Beijing is still often a dustbowl from March to May. It is not unusual to see women cover their heads and faces with silk scarves for protection.

Types of Tea

Tea is the most popular non-alcoholic beverage in China. There are four types: green tea, black tea, oolong tea, and the very rare white tea. The differences among the first three lie not in the type of plant, but in the way the leaves are processed.

Green tea is the most common. It is produced from freshly picked, unfermented tea leaves, which are first steamed, then dried over a charcoal fire. The most famous green tea in China is known as Dragon Well and is grown on the hillsides of Hangzhou.

Black tea – which the Chinese call "red tea" – is made from fermented tea leaves, which explains its darker color. The leaves are first allowed to wither, or dry, in bamboo trays. Next they are rolled and sifted. This process bruises the leaves, thus encouraging fermentation. With oxidation, the leaves turn even darker in color and acquire a recognizable tea odor. When the leaves have fermented to the desired level, they are roasted to stop fermentation and to destroy bacteria.

Oolong tea is partially fermented, making it halfway between black and green tea in flavor. Once the edges of the leaves turn brown, the fermentation process is stopped by roasting the leaves in a pan.

White tea is made from the buds of a very rare type of tea plant. The tea, which is harvested for only a few days a year, is very subtle in flavor.

In addition to these four kinds of tea, there are multiple variations, including scented teas. To produce these, dried flowers are added to green and

• •

oolong teas. The most popular of the scented teas is jasmine.

Careers for the Younger Generation

As China's economy develops, an increasing number of career options is open to the country's young and ambitious. Expanded options, however, often come at the cost of decreased job security. Gone are the days when a job with a state-owned company was considered an "iron rice-bowl," that is, a meal ticket for life. State-owned companies have to compete to survive in the new market economy, and private enterprise is growing. Today, college graduates dream of pursuing white-collar work in banking, foreign or joint-venture enterprises, and high-tech industries. These young people represent an emerging middle class in Chinese society.

IT Industries in China

In recent years many high-tech firms have sprung up in China, especially in Beijing, Shenzhen (which lies across the border from Hong Kong), and the

• •

region around Shanghai. In Beijing, most of China's burgeoning software companies are concentrated in a small area called *zhong guan cun*. Its prominence derives from the fact that Beijing is home to many of the country's most prestigious universities and colleges, as well as to government research institutions. This vast pool of talents is the biggest asset of *zhong guan cun*. The success of Shenzhen is due to the city's status as a special economic zone with flexible policies and to its proximity to Hong Kong, while the greater Shanghai metropolitan area in recent years has begun to attract many chip-makers and notebook manufacturers from Taiwan.

Harbin

Harbin is the capital of China's northernmost province, Heilongjiang. The city derives its name from the Manchu word for "honor" or "fame." Harbin's geography and history lend it a distinctly Russian flavor. In the late nineteenth century, the Russians built a railway line from Vladivostok to Harbin. Several decades later, after the Russian Revolution of 1917, the city saw an influx of refugees from Siberia. The Russian imprint is still visible in much of the city's architecture. Today, there is

• •

flourishing trade and cross-border tourism between Harbin and the Russian far eastern region.

Harbin's main tourist attraction is its Ice Lantern Festival. This takes place every winter from January 5 to February 15. Whimsical ice sculptures are displayed in the main park and illuminated at night.

pu tong hua hen nan, or Chinese Adjectives

Chinese adjectives are inherently contrastive. For this reason, adjectives are not used on their own in Chinese when no contrast is intended. To cancel out the contrast, a qualifier such as *hen* ("very") is added to the adjective: *pu tong hua **hen** nan* ("Chinese is *very* difficult") as opposed to simply, *pu tong hua nan*. If you say *pu tong hua nan*, you are actually saying that Mandarin is difficult *compared to some other language*, whether or not that language is mentioned. The comparison or contrast is implicit. To make a blanket statement with no comparison implied, you must add "very" or a similar qualifier, such as "extraordinarily," "a little," and so on. This rule of thumb applies not only to *nan*, but to most other adjectives as well – for example, *pu tong hua hen rong yi* ("Chinese is very easy").

● ●

China is a country of many dialects. There are seven major groups: Mandarin, Wu, Xiang, Gan, Kejia or Hakka, Min, and Yue (Cantonese). The main differences among them are in pronunciation and vocabulary, although there are differences in syntax as well.

The most important and widespread of these dialects is Mandarin, which is the standard spoken language in China. Approximately 70 percent of the population speaks some variety of Mandarin as a mother tongue. Standard Chinese is based on the dialect spoken by the residents of Beijing, China's capital since the thirteenth century. Some of the so-called "dialects" – some linguists classify them as different languages – are mutually unintelligible. For example, someone from the province of Guangdong in the deep south will not be able to communicate with his compatriots from the north, unless they both resort to Mandarin. It is known as "Mandarin" in English because it was the lingua franca among scholar-officials, or Mandarins, in pre-modern China.

Unlike Mandarin, or *pu tong hua*, the term *zhong wen* in its narrow sense refers to the written Chinese language used by about 95 percent of the population

Dialects (continued)

• •

in China. It should be noted that *zhong wen* implies the *written* form of Chinese; the many dialects, including Mandarin, represent a variety of *spoken* forms. (Colloquially, *zhong wen* can also refer to spoken Chinese, but *wen* properly means "written language.") Because *zhong wen* is the standard written language, it is possible for people from all over the country to communicate with one another in writing. However, with the increasing spread of education and mass media, particularly film and TV, more and more people throughout China also understand and speak Mandarin. Because the Chinese government discourages the use of dialects, some of them are in danger of becoming displaced by Mandarin all together.

Purpose or Motion: *shang da xue* vs. *qu da xue*

wo shang da xue, means "I'm a college student," or "I go to college." Notice that you use *shang*, rather than *qu*. In colloquial Chinese *shang* often has the meaning "to go." The difference between *shang* and *qu*, which is the standard equivalent of "to go," is that *shang* connotes the activity associated with a specific location rather than the simple act of going there. Therefore, *shang da xue* means

• •

to *study* at the university, whereas *qu da xue* merely suggests *movement* towards the university. The purpose of the action is left unspecified. One could go to the university (*qu da xue*) to visit a friend, for instance. For the same reason, *shang fan dian* means "to eat at a restaurant" rather than simply "to go to a restaurant."

Classifiers, or "Measure Words"

A distinguishing feature of modern Chinese is its use of classifiers, also known as "measure words." In classical Chinese they were largely absent. In modern Chinese, however, when describing quantity, you need not only the appropriate nouns and numerals, but also the corresponding classifiers. For example, to say "*a* book," you say *yi **ben** shu*; "two people" is *liang **ge** ren*. The choice of measure word is usually determined by the nature of the item in question.

ge is perhaps the most versatile classifier. It can be used as a somewhat generic measure word with a wide variety of countable nouns, especially in collo-quial Chinese; in formal Chinese, however, more

• •

specific classifiers are preferred. For instance, when speaking informally, you could get away with *yi ge ren* ("a person" or "one person"), *yi ge fan dian* ("a restaurant"), *yi ge yin hang* ("a bank"). Most measure words, however, are much more restrictive and can be used only with specific nouns or categories of nouns.

Some common measure words follow.

- *wei*: This measure word is used to refer to people. It's more polite than *ge*. Therefore, to show respect to a friend, you say, *yi **wei** peng you,* rather than, *yi **ge** peng you.* The original meaning of the word *wei* is "seat" – by implication, it means the person occupying the seat of honor.

- *zhang* is used to refer to objects with wide flat surfaces, such as sofas, desks, or beds: *yi zhang sha fa* ("a sofa"), *liang zhang zhuo zi* ("two desks"), *san zhang chuang* "(three beds"). The original meaning of the word is "to stretch."

Classifiers, or "Measure Words" (continued)

- *ba* refers to objects that you can get a grip on, for instance, chairs: *liang ba yi zi* ("two chairs"). Its original meaning is "handle."

- *tou* applies to things that have heads, like animals: *yi tou niu* ("an ox," "a bull," or "a cow") or *yi tou zhu* ("a pig"). Not all animals take this measure word, however.

- *ben* is used primarily to refer to books: *wu ben shu* ("five books").

- *jia*:   The original meaning of the word is "home." As a measure word, it is used with the names for institutions and establishments closely associated with the physical structures that house them, such as banks, restaurants, or libraries.

Chinese has well over one hundred fifty measure words. Of these, at least a hundred are relatively common, and dozens are used in daily conversation.

• •

bai jiu is the generic name for many different types of distilled spirits. They are called *bai jiu,* or "white liquor," because they are colorless. Most are made from grains – often sorghum, a type of millet. The grains are steamed and yeast is added, to aid in the fermentation process.

Most of the liquor consumed by the Chinese is made in the Sichuan province. The most famous *bai jiu* from Sichuan is known as *wu liang ye,* meaning "five grain liquid" or "five grain nectar." As its name suggests, it is made from five varieties of grains: "regular" rice, glutinous rice, wheat, sorghum, and corn. It is slightly sweet and highly fragrant.

Shanxi province, near Beijing, is famous for its *fen jiu,* which is made from local sorghum. Yeast made from wheat and peas is added, and the sorghum is steamed and buried underground for twenty-one days to allow fermentation. More yeast is then added, and the mixture is fermented and distilled again. After blending, the liquor is ready to bottle.

Another well-known variety of *bai jiu* is called *er guo tou.* It's particularly popular with the working

• •

class in northern China. The most famous of all the white liquors is *mao tai*, which is named after the town in Guizhou Province where it is produced.

Peking Duck

Perhaps the most famous dish associated with the capital of China, Peking duck is prepared in several steps, all of which ensure its unique flavor. The duck is raised on farms around Beijing (formerly called "Peking") on a diet of grain and soybean paste. The mature fattened duck is slaughtered, then lacquered with molasses; air is pumped under the skin to separate it from the carcass, after which the duck is boiled, dried, and finally roasted over a fruitwood fire.

Quanjude Restaurant in Beijing, which dates back to 1864, is *the* place to try this delectable dish. The entire feast consists of two main stages. First the boneless meat and skin are served with a plum sauce, scallions, and crepes. Then comes the duck soup, made from the bones and other parts of the duck. Although the most authentic version can be had only at *Quanjude*, Peking duck is widely available throughout Beijing.

Hotels

• •

There is a wide range of tourist accommodations in China, all the way from budget guesthouses to luxurious five-star hotels. In most big cities, high end hotel prices are comparable to those in Europe and North America. The luxury market is dominated by familiar international chains such as Hilton, Sheraton, Ritz-Carlton, and Four Seasons. For the frugally-minded, it's possible to find university dormitories and government-run guesthouses. However, many, although not all, are off-limits to international travelers. Western-style youth hostels and bed-and-breakfasts are still rare.

For travelers in the know, it is sometimes possible to stay at one of the five-star hotels while avoiding the exorbitant rate. Some of them have discounts available for the asking, but you must inquire, as these discounts are not always advertised.

• •

As the Chinese standard of living continues to rise, dining out is becoming increasingly common. Many, if not all, of the popular restaurants in the big cities are privately owned. These range from mom-and-pop holes-in-the-wall to vast, opulently-decked-out multi-story gastronomical emporia. In fact, size seems in direct proportion to flash and price. Some of the glitzy restaurants feature live orchestras and private banquet rooms. Patrons are invited to inspect live seafood in water tanks on the first floor while waitresses, most of whom come from the provinces, take the orders.

There is a vast array of food to be had, from regional cuisine to international fare. In Beijing and Shanghai, virtually all types of Chinese and foreign food can be found, although Chinese dishes are still the most popular. Two trends, regionalism and cosmopolitanism, are emerging in the restaurant scene. Authentic regional cuisine is on the rise, but so is fusion food. Foie gras and sashimi have both made their way onto some of the fancier restaurant menus.

Hainan and Sanya
● ●

Hainan is a large tropical island off the coast of southern China. Its yearly average temperature is seventy-eight degrees Fahrenheit. From March to November the island is shrouded in heat and humidity. Hainan is famous for its tropical plants and crops: coconuts, pepper, coffee, and rubber, among others. Many of the farms on Hainan were founded by ethnic Chinese from Southeast Asia, the descendants of emigrants who resettled in their ancestral homeland after the waves of anti-Chinese feeling in Indonesia and Malaysia in the 1960s. Since there is little heavy industry, pollution is minimal. Until 1988 Hainan was part of Guangdong Province. The island was elevated to provincial status when the Chinese government decided to open it up to foreign investors. Its capital city is Haikou, on the northern coastline. During peak season, Hainan is a favored site for tourists.

The most popular tourist destination, however, is Sanya in the south. Blessed with miles of excellent beaches, it's one of the most well-known winter resorts in China.

"Hotel" - *jiu dian* vs. *lü guan*

• •

As you know, Chinese has multiple dialects, which can result in several names for the same thing. A second word for "hotel" is *lü guan* rather than *jiu dian*. *lü guan* is more common in the north, *jiu dian* in the south. Their connotations may differ as well.

In Mandarin *lü guan* is the generic word for "hotel." This term covers the whole range of tourist accommodations from the simplest inn to the glitziest five-star hotel.

jiu dian, on the other hand, almost always refers to big, fancy establishments. In addition, it generally occurs as part of a hotel name. *jiu dian* literally means "wine shop"; it originally designated a traditional Chinese-style pub where rice wine or other kinds of alcohol and simple food are served, and customers sit on long narrow benches around rectangular tables. Then, in the 1980s, developers from Hong Kong built the first modern international tourist hotels in China. Since these hotels were located in the south, the term *jiu dian* was often applied to them. For this reason, *jiu dian* sounds vaguely Cantonese to Mandarin speakers, although today they may use it as well, to refer to a top-quality hotel.

Part Three   *go*Chinese · Mandarin

Chang'an Avenue and Tian'anmen Square

• •

Chang'an Avenue is Beijing's answer to the Champs Elysées. It is one of the main thorough-fares in Beijing. Government offices, monuments, and museums sit side-by-side along this multi-lane artery. The retail epicenter Wangfujing is a stone's throw away. At the heart of Chang'an Avenue is the immense windswept Tian'anmen Square. Both the avenue and the square were created by Mao Zedong in the 1950s. The square is named after the Tian'anmen Gate in the Forbidden City, from which Chairman Mao proclaimed the founding of the People's Republic of China in 1949. Tian'anmen Square is fraught with economic and political significance, as many momentous events in modern Chinese history took place there and in the surrounding area.

• •

China has diplomatic relations with more than one hundred countries. Most foreign embassies in Beijing are concentrated in two areas: Jianguomenwai and Sanlitun, east and northeast of the Forbidden City, respectively. It is not unusual to see long lines of Chinese outside the tightly-guarded compounds, waiting for visas to study or work abroad.

Sanlitun is also home to Beijing's well-known "bar street" – or rather "streets," as there is now a "Sanlitun North Street" and a "Sanlitun South Street," both of which are highly popular among tourists. Scores of bars and nightclubs line the sides of these narrow dusty roads. Because of their proximity to the diplomatic quarters, the variously-themed bars and clubs cater to a largely foreign clientele.

Wangfujing Avenue

• •

Along with Chang'an Avenue, Wangfujing is one of the most famous street addresses not only in Beijing, but all over China. Most of the older department stores, traditional shops, boutiques, and bookstores can be found on this block. After a recent makeover, however, the street is now almost unrecognizable to those who visited it even a few years ago. Locals and tourists throng the area, especially on weekends. Part of Wangfujing has been closed to vehicular traffic. Life-size sculptures depicting old Beijing urban life dot the pedestrian zone. While it's no longer the most prestigious or fashionable shopping area in the city, it's still the most famous.

• •

Lying northwest of the Forbidden City, Beihai Park is the former playground of the Manchu emperors. Artificial hills, picturesque pavilions, and colorful temples compose the landscape. Half of the park is a man-made lake. The most prominent landmark of the park is the bulbous White Pagoda. Built in a Tibetan architectural style, it commemorates a visit by the Dalai Lama. Another well-known feature of the park is the Painted Gallery. Idyllic sceneries are depicted on the beams of the winding covered walkway. Equally well known is the Nine Dragon Screen, whose sixteen by eighty-eight foot wall is made of colored glazed tiles. Beihai Park is also famous for its restaurant, which serves the favorite recipes of the Manchu emperors and empresses. Prices, as one can imagine, are high.

guo vs. *le*

Note the following sentence: *wo shang ge xing qi lai* **guo** *zhe jia fan dian.* ("I came to this restaurant last week.") In this statement you used *guo* instead of *le* because you were explaining why you know the food is good at the restaurant – it's because you've tried it. You were at the restaurant last

guo vs. *le* *(continued)*

● ●

week. The word *guo* suggests the *experience* of having done something. In other words, with *guo* the emphasis is on the present implication of a past action rather than on its completion. On the other hand, if you say: *wo shang ge xing qi lai* **le** *zhe jia fan dian*, the focus is on the *completion* of the action. Perhaps it was something you were supposed to do, and you did it. You completed the task.

Here's another example: You know that Sam has been to Beijing, so you think he should know what the weather is like there. You could then say, *Sam, ni qu* **guo** *bei jing. Bei jing de tian qi zen me yang?* ("Sam, you have been to Beijing. How is Beijing's weather?") The particle *le* would be incorrect here. *le* would emphasize that Sam completed the trip instead of having had the experience of being in Beijing. For this reason, if Sam is a traveling salesman and was supposed to stop in Beijing and you'd simply like to know whether he's done that, then you would ask, *Sam, ni qu Bei jing* **le** *ma?* ("Sam, did you go to Beijing?")

More on *le*

• •

For an English speaker, it may take some getting used to the fact that Chinese has no tenses. Many grammatical features that English speakers take for granted, such as tenses (past, present, future), number (singular or plural), and articles ("the," "a," "an,"), do not apply to Chinese. Instead, Chinese has its own unique set of grammatical character-istics. One is the aspect marker *le*.

le is easily confused with the equivalent of the English past tense. Rather, *le* signifies the comp-letion of an action *regardless of time*. In other words, it is possible to use *le* to refer to the future completion of an action – for example, *ming tian wo kan **le** dianying qu kan wo de peng you* ("Tomorrow after I see the film – literally, after I *complete* seeing the film – I'm going to see my friend.")

By the same token, one does not automatically use *le* when describing past actions. Native speakers of Chinese distinguish between background and foreground information. *le* is used for foreground, but not for background. In conveying background information, the speaker is merely setting the scene of a past event, and *le* is omitted. In a description of foreground information, *le* is needed. For example,

● ●

consider the following pair of Chinese sentences and their English equivalents:

> *zuo tian wan shang wo men qu fan dian chi fan.*
> "Last night we went to a restaurant to eat."

> *fan dian li ren hen duo, suo yi wo men deng **le** hen jiu.*
> "There were many people in the restaurant, so we waited a long time."

Notice the absence of *le* in the first Chinese sentence ("Last night we went to a restaurant to eat") and the presence of *le* in the second (" ... we waited a long time"). "We waited a long time" is the focus of the narration, or the foreground information. That is why the speaker uses *le*. Everything prior to that clause is the background information. The act of going to a restaurant is *not* the emphasis of the speaker's narration. Therefore the particle *le* is omitted.

gan bei!

• •

In China as elsewhere, large quantities of alcohol are sometimes consumed on various festive occasions. The level of formality and the elaborateness of the toasts depend on the status and the number of the guests. Generally, the more elevated the guests' status, or the greater their number, the more formal and elaborate the toasts will be. The most common toast at Chinese banquets is probably *gan bei!* or, "Bottoms up!" (literally, "Make the cups dry!"). Highly formulaic and literary Chinese is often used to add dignity to the occasions. Speeches frequently end with an exhortation to raise the cup and down the drink, which is often *mao tai*, one of the "white liquors." Cognac or other kinds of foreign liquor are also popular.

Omission of Pronouns

The Chinese language is highly dependent on context. One example of this characteristic is the omission of pronouns. English-speakers may occasionally omit pronouns when speaking very informally. For example, they may ask, "Need any help?" or, "Want some dessert?" However, this is much more common in Chinese. In Chinese, pronouns can

Omission of Pronouns (continued)

• •

usually be omitted as long as there is no possi-
bility of confusion. For example, if someone asks
you in Chinese where you are going, you can leave
out the pronoun "I" in your answer without causing
any misunderstanding. Likewise, if you are clearly
addressing just one person, you can ask, "Have a
fever?" without any ambiguity as to whom is meant.

Pronouns are also omitted for social reasons.
When addressing one's superior, it is a good idea
to use his or her title rather than the pronoun *ni*
("you"). The more formal *nin*, however, is perfectly
respectful and can be used in place of the title.

Special Economic Zones and Industrial Parks

One of the most important engines driving the
Chinese economy in the last twenty years has been
the formation of so-called "special economic zones"
along China's coast. Such zones were given tax
breaks and other preferential treatment to enable
them to attract investment from overseas. The
infusion of capital and technology, along with the
abundant supply of cheap labor, became a foolproof
recipe for success. The most spectacular example is

• •

Shenzhen, located between Mainland China and Hong Kong. Once a sleepy border crossing, it was transformed into a thriving metropolis almost overnight. Thanks to many such zones, today Chinese products can be found on department store shelves all over the world.

Two decades ago, when the country was still trying to shake off the communist orthodoxy of the planned economy, the special economic zones were an important, albeit sometimes controversial, testing ground for an alternative economic system. Essentially, they were experiments in a free-market economy. Now, many of the special economic zones are seeking to upgrade from manufacturing to high tech business. Gleaming office buildings and immaculate industrial parks, many built with Taiwanese capital, stand as a symbol of China's ever-increasing economic importance.

Women in Business

• •

Since it was founded in 1949, the People's Republic of China has officially embraced gender equality. Practices such as prostitution and concubinage were outlawed, and the new constitution provided for equal rights for women in all areas of life. Chairman Mao famously said, "Times have changed. Men and women are equal. Women can accomplish whatever men can," and even more famously, "Women hold up half the sky." Women were encouraged to work outside the home. As a result, women can be found in all walks of life. In certain professions, for instance medicine, there are equal numbers of women and men. In others, such as elementary and secondary education, women generally outnumber men.

One exception is the business world. While some successful, high-profile businesswomen can be found, most women still occupy entry-level or subsidiary positions. Women, mostly young and attractive, requisite qualities as described in want ads, fill the ranks of secretaries and receptionists. The business culture in China is still very much male dominated.

• •

Seventy-five miles to the northwest of Shanghai, Suzhou was an important cultural center during the Ming and Qing dynasties, which lasted from the fourteenth through the nineteenth century. Suzhou is especially renowned for its many traditional gardens which date from this era. Though not as grand as the vast imperial parks in Beijing, the small gardens in Suzhou were the retreats of the city's many scholar-officials during the Ming and Qing dynasties. Much thought went into the design of these gardens, which often featured pavilions, ponds, and stone bridges. Fantastically eroded stones for rock gardens were harvested from the bottom of nearby Lake Tai. Unlike in western gardens, plantings did not play a predominant role in the design.

Much of the charm of the city came from its dense network of waterways. Unfortunately, many of the small canals and rivers were paved over. With tourism booming, efforts are being made to restore some of the surrounding small towns, which are miniatures of Suzhou and feature the same combinations of landscaped gardens, stone arch bridges, and canalscapes. Along with Hangzhou, which lies at the end of China's Grand Canal, Suzhou is one of the most popular tourist cities in China. Its many

• •

Buddhist and Daoist temples, historic sites, traditional scholar-gardens, and canals attract busloads of tourists every day. Both Hangzhou and Suzhou are located in China's prosperous Yangtze River delta, which is known as China's "land of fish and rice." The natural abundance and material affluence of the two cities gave rise to the old Chinese saying, "[there's] heaven on high and Suzhou and Hangzhou on earth."

Today Suzhou is also an economic powerhouse. Its suburbs have become especially popular with Taiwanese high-tech firms. The Suzhou metropolitan area is rapidly becoming one of the world's most important manufacturing centers of laptop computers.

Interpreters

As more and more international companies invest in China, the demand for interpreters is growing accordingly. Most interpreters in China are graduates of foreign-language departments at Chinese colleges and universities. The curriculum for foreign-language majors can be quite rigorous, with heavy emphasis on grammar and theoretical knowledge of the target languages. Twenty years ago many students went through their course of study without having ever met a single native speaker. This situation has improved considerably during the past two decades. Today, many so-called "foreign experts" are hired to teach foreign languages, and Chinese students have more opportunities to study abroad.

Foreign-language programs have also become quite common on Chinese television. These changes have resulted in a higher level of competence among Chinese interpreters. In addition to colleges and universities, many "evening schools" – as continuing education is called in China – offer foreign-language classes. Their graduates can also be found among the ranks of interpreters.

Besides English and Japanese, interpreters of Korean are also in great demand, especially in Shandong Peninsula and Jilin Province, a reflection of the growing presence of Korean businesses in China.

Flower Appreciation

• •

Every year, as various kinds of flowers come into bloom, people in China go on excursions to admire them. The suburbs of Nanjing and Suzhou are especially famous for their plum blossoms, which blanket the surrounding hills each spring. Farther to the north, Luoyang attracts many tourists when the peonies are in bloom in April. In the fall, parks put on chrysanthemum shows. The flowers are trained or arranged to form spectacular topiaries and abstract patterns. Plum blossoms, peonies, and chrysanthemums are popular in China partly because of the qualities associated with them. Plum blossoms symbolize nobility and purity; showy peonies, prosperity; and hardy chrysanthemums are particularly respected for their endurance.

In traditional China, flowers also inspired many poets and painters. The scholar literati, of course, did not need to venture far to appreciate flowers. Their carefully laid-out gardens provided the ideal setting for them to get together, drink rice wine, and compose poetry. These occasions often contained an element of competition, as difficult or obscure rhymes were chosen and friends attempted to outdo one another in poetic virtuosity. If a friend was absent, the poems would be sent to him. Many court

● ●

painters specialized in the "flower and bird" genre, which, unlike literati painting, was known for its attention to realistic detail.

The Palace Museum in Beijing

Most museums in China derive their core collections from archeological finds. One of the notable exceptions is the Palace Museum in Beijing. The Palace Museum is housed in the vast Forbidden City, home and administrative center of the Ming and Qing emperors for well over five hundred years. During this time (1368-1911), it was occupied by not only the emperors and their families, but hundreds of court ladies and palace eunuchs. It was, however, forbidden to the common people; even the highest civil and military leaders could not enter without good reason. All four sides were protected by a moat and high walls, almost 33 feet high, that slant inward from the base, making them extremely difficult to climb. The entire complex covers 182 acres and contains 9,999 buildings, palaces, halls, and courtyards. After China's last emperor abdicated from the throne and vacated the palace in the early 1900s, the Forbidden City became a museum and was opened to the public.

Today, both the architectural ensemble and the former imperial collection of art are crowd-pleasers. The art works, which consist of bronzes, paintings, ceramics, and decorative objects, reflect the tastes of China's former rulers. UNESCO has designated the entire complex a World Heritage Site.

In addition to the better-known original in Beijing, Taipei also has a National Palace Museum. This curious coexistence and rivalry is a product of China's turbulent modern history. On the eve of its retreat to Taiwan, the Nationalist government removed thousands of crates of relics belonging to the Palace Museum in Beijing to the outskirts of Taipei. A complex of pale yellow buildings in traditional Chinese style was built, and the National Palace Museum opened in 1965. Today the museum boasts of having a collection superior to its rival in Beijing.

● ●

Luoyang, in Henan province, is one of the most ancient cities in China. It was the capital of thirteen dynasties. During Buddhism's heyday, Luoyang was also home to thirteen hundred Buddhist temples. Today, however, the city's past glory lingers mainly in historical records. Although there are some sites to be seen within the city limits, tourists invariably flock to the Longmen Caves on the outskirts of the city. There, more than one hundred thousand Buddhist images and statues were carved into the cliff overlooking the Yi River. Most of the Buddhist art works in the Longmen Caves date from the fifth through ninth centuries.

Luoyang is also famous throughout China for its peonies. The city has a long history of growing these flowers, and their sheer variety is unrivaled throughout the world. Every year from April 15 to April 25, the city holds a peony festival.

Gift-Giving / Hospitality

Gift-giving in China is traditionally associated with specific festivals or social occasions. For instance, at Chinese New Year it is customary to

• •

give small children pocket-money wrapped in red paper embossed with gold characters. During the Mid-Autumn Festival, elaborately packaged moon cakes are exchanged among friends and relatives. To celebrate the birthday of an elderly person, well-wishers traditionally give noodles, as their long stringy shape symbolizes longevity. Some items, however, are not appropriate as gifts: clocks, for example, are considered highly unsuitable, because the phrase for "giving the gift of a clock" – *song zhong*, sounds exactly the same as the phrase meaning "attending upon a dying parent or senior family member."

Chinese people are less inclined to invite casual friends home than Americans, simply because most city-dwellers live in small apartments. They are therefore more likely to socialize in restaurants or other public spaces. In this case, the standard gesture of hospitality is to argue over the check after a meal or before a show. To the more traditionally-minded Chinese, the practice of splitting a check is a foreign concept, although it is gaining acceptance among westernized young people. When Chinese people do invite guests over, a common hostess gift is a basket of fresh fruit.

● ●

If you walk into a bookstore in China, you're likely to see swarms of elementary and high school students with their parents in tow looking for various kinds of study guides, which they hope will help them get into the school of their choice. Indeed, some smaller bookstores seem to carry nothing but reference works aimed at those preparing for the all-important and very competitive high school and college entrance exams. Sometimes an entire floor of a bookstore is devoted to these books. School-age children probably represent the most lucrative demographic group for the Chinese publishing industry.

Other children's books sell very well, too. Harry Potter has an enthusiastic readership among Chinese children. Their parents, however, are another matter. Often they forbid their children to waste their time on "idle" reading materials. It seems likely that even Harry Potter is outsold by the ubiquitous study guides.

Other popular categories of books include computer references and stock investment guides, which are always very prominently displayed. The book trade used to be dominated by the state-owned

• •

xinhua (New China) group, but in recent years, private bookstores have appeared all over China. They vary greatly in size, quality of service, and range of merchandise.

Classical Music

When people say *gu dian yin yue*, they are usually referring to western classical music. It is considered "high, elegant art," or *gao ya yi shu* in Chinese. Therefore, it enjoys considerable cachet and popularity among the urban educated classes. Western orchestras can be found in the cities of Beijing, Shanghai, and Guangzhou. Beijing and Shanghai each have several orchestras. Shanghai, in fact, boasts of having the oldest western orchestra in East Asia, a legacy of its semi-colonial past. The municipal council in the so-called International Settlement in Shanghai set up this orchestra at the end of the nineteenth century. The first generation of classical musicians in China was trained under the tutelage of western conductors.

• •

During the Cultural Revolution (1966-1976), western classical music was labeled "decadent bourgeois art" and was in effect banned. When the Philadelphia Orchestra visited China at the invitation of Chairman Mao's wife in 1973, it was the first western orchestra to do so. The visit was considered big news, and both Chinese and American politicians dubbed the orchestra the "symphony ambassador." After the Cultural Revolution, western classical music made a comeback and is now more popular than ever. The Chinese government actively promotes it and is especially proud of the fact that young Chinese musicians routinely win prizes at international competitions.

The Chinese Educational System

Primary education in China lasts six years, junior and senior high another six. In addition to regular school hours, additional sessions are held in the evenings and on weekends. These classes are not for the academically challenged, everyone takes them. A Chinese student's schedule, therefore, can be quite grueling. Newspaper editorials routinely call for schools to lessen the burden on students, but these appeals have little effect. Parents and students may complain about the workload, but that does not stop them from hiring tutors and cramming evening classes and extracurricular activities into the schedule.

Primary and secondary education are subsidized by the state, but schools often charge "sponsorship fees," which can be quite high. Higher education is no longer free, either. To help college students and their parents, various scholarships and loans are available. A fairly recent development is the rise of private schools. They have sprung up all over China, but particularly along China's prosperous eastern seaboard. Compared with public schools, private schools often enjoy superior facilities and attract better qualified teachers. However, the most prestigious schools are the so-called "key schools," which are all public. Only the most academically gifted need apply. Admission is extremely competitive and is widely viewed as a ticket to future success at the college level and beyond.

• • • • • • • • • • • • • • • • • • • •

If you go to China, the chances are that every morning you'll see armies of people in parks, in schoolyards, or on street corners, doing their daily exercises, usually to the accompaniment of rather loud music. Various types of *tai ji* are particularly popular with older people and women. School-age children, factory workers, and company employees often get a mid-morning exercise break, during which they do calisthenics. Students also perform a set of exercises designed to protect their eyesight; to this end, they massage the various acupuncture pressure points around the eyes for about five to ten minutes. Jogging and weight-training, by contrast, are not nearly as popular or common as they are in America. Aerobics is. Many western-style gyms have sprung up in big cities. Young urban professionals, who are often health-conscious and have the requisite disposable income, flock to these fashionable health clubs.

Despite what a casual visitor to the country may see, obesity, coronary conditions, and diseases such as diabetes are on the rise. Ironically, as the country becomes more prosperous, certain health problems have also become more prevalent. For this reason, diabetes and heart conditions are known as *fu gui bing*, or "diseases of affluence."

Tourist Souvenirs

Unless they are "off the beaten track," travelers to China will find it hard to avoid tourist shops. Antique stores and souvenir stands often overflow into the streets. Increasingly, tourism is becoming an important source of revenue.

The souvenirs available depend on the locales. In Xi'an, for example, it is difficult to miss reproductions of Tang dynasty pottery. The brightly colored earthenware is known as *tang san cai*, or Tang-style tricolored glazed ware. The name *san cai* stems from the predominant glazes of brown, yellow, and green. Camels with bearded Central Asian merchants on the their backs are a frequent theme. Hand-embroidered shoes and pouches are also common.

In Suzhou, silk scarves and sandalwood fans are ubiquitous. Suzhou is also famous for its fine embroidery, particularly its *shuang mian xiu*, or "double-embroidery." A highly skilled artisan can

• •

embroider two different designs, one on each side of the fabric, which is usually silk – for instance, a Persian cat on one side, and a Pekingese on the other.

Of course, handicrafts are not the only thing for sale. In Beijing, T-shirts emblazoned with pictures of the Great Wall, the Temple of Heaven, or other famous sights are offered by the many souvenir peddlers plying their business around the capital.

Saying Good-bye

Bidding someone farewell is an elaborate social ritual in China. A considerable length of time may elapse between the time one says good-bye and the time one actually leaves. The host or hostess's first response is invariably, "Oh, please stay a bit longer." And no host or hostess would be content just seeing guests to the door. In fact, that would be perceived as downright cold and inhospitable. More often than not, the host will insist on accompanying his or her guest to the bus stop or waiting with the guest for a taxi. In fact, most hosts go even further and wait until the guest is out of sight – that is, until the bus or taxi has driven away.

In traditional China, leave-taking for a long separation was even more ceremonious. Often a series of farewell banquets was hosted in the departing friend's honor, and heartfelt poems were exchanged. When the actual day of departure arrived, people would travel a significant distance with the departing friend, until final farewells were exchanged. Classical Chinese poetry abounds in works depicting poignant moments when one's most intimate friends are departing for distant destinations, perhaps never to return. Today, of course, departures are less likely to be final, and communication is much easier; nevertheless, leave-taking is still much more formal than in the West.

SIMON & SCHUSTER'S

PIMSLEUR

· ·

Pimsleur programs are also available in the following languages:

- Albanian
- Arabic (Eastern)
- Arabic (Egyptian)
- Armenian (Eastern)
- Armenian (Western)
- Chinese (Cantonese)
- Chinese (Mandarin)
- Croatian
- Czech
- Danish
- Dari (Persian)
- Dutch
- Farsi (Persian)
- French
- German
- Greek
- Haitian Creole
- Hebrew
- Hindi
- Hungarian
- Indonesian
- Irish

- Italian
- Japanese
- Korean
- Lithuanian
- Norwegian
- Ojibwe
- Polish
- Portuguese (Brazilian)
- Portuguese (European)
- Romanian
- Russian
- Spanish *(for Children & Adults)*
- Swahili
- Swedish
- Swiss German
- Tagalog
- Thai
- Turkish
- Twi
- Ukrainian
- Urdu
- Vietnamese

English as a Second Language (ESL) programs are available for native speakers of the following languages:

- Arabic
- Chinese (Cantonese)
- Chinese (Mandarin)
- Farsi (Persian)
- French
- German
- Haitian Creole

- Hindi
- Italian
- Korean
- Portuguese
- Russian
- Spanish
- Vietnamese